HOLY
yoga

HOLY

Exercise for the Christian Body and Soul

yoga

Brooke Boon

FaithWords

NEW YORK   BOSTON   NASHVILLE

Neither this exercise program nor any other exercise program should be followed without first consulting a health-care professional. If you have any special conditions requiring attention, you should consult with your health-care professional regularly regarding possible modification of the program contained in this book.

Illustrations by Greg Hansen.

Unless otherwise noted, Scriptures are taken from the HOLY BIBLE: NEW INTERNATIONAL VERSION®. Copyright © 1973, 1978, 1984 by International Bible Society. Used by permission of Zondervan Publishing House. All rights reserved.
Scriptures noted The Message are taken from The Message. Copyright © 1993, 1994, 1995, 1996, 2000, 2001, 2002. Used by permission of NavPress Publishing Group.
Scriptures noted TEV are taken from TODAY'S ENGLISH VERSION. Copyright © American Bible Society 1966, 1971, 1976, 1992.

FaithWords
Hachette Book Group USA
237 Park Avenue
New York, NY 10017

Visit our Web site at www.faithwords.com.

Book design by Fearn Cutler de Vicq.

Printed in the United States of America

FIRST EDITION: AUGUST 2007
10 9 8 7 6 5 4 3 2 1

The FaithWords name and logo are trademarks of Hachette Book Group USA.

Library of Congress Cataloging-in-Publication Data
Boon, Brooke.
  Holy yoga : exercise for the Christian body and soul / Brooke Boon. —1st ed.
    p. cm.
Includes bibliographical references and index.
ISBN-13: 978-0-446-69915-0
ISBN-10: 0-446-69915-2
1. Christianity and yoga.   I. Title.
BR128.Y63B66 2007
248.4'6—dc22
                    2006101601

To my heavenly Father:
I dedicate this work, along with the rest of my life, to You.

To my beloved family:
Jarrett—my husband, best friend, and God-given angel.
Thank you for loving me and for giving me the gift
of an earthly forever.

And to my children, Jory, Jace, and Brynn:
You are my ultimate blessings and my greatest rewards.
May God bless you all with passion for Him
as the center of your lives
And grant you His peace while in pursuit.

I love you all.

Contents

Part Three
The Postures

Acknowledgments

With utmost respect and admiration I thank Rachelle Gardner, without whom this project would have never seen the light of day. Thank you for capturing Holy Yoga with such perfection. You are a joy and His gift of you to this project is immeasurable.

Thank you to Steve Laube for believing in and supporting this project at every turn.

Thank you to Greg Hansen for capturing the beauty and simplicity of Holy Yoga in your illustrations.

To all of my students: thank you for inspiring me every day through your passion for Holy Yoga and your peace while in the presence of the Lord. And my deepest gratitude to the first Holy Yoga teachers for your fire and dedication to spreading the love of worshiping the Lord through this ministry.

Thank you to Pastor Bob Rognlien for his wisdom and teachings on loving God with heart, soul, mind, and strength in his book, *Experiential Worship*. Special thanks to Larry Payne for his knowledge and insight on yoga's many physical benefits.

Finally, thank you to Holly Halverson and the amazing team at FaithWords who embraced *Holy Yoga* for all that it will do in bringing people in to authentic connection with Christ.

To all my friends, new and old—my heartfelt thanks. Not to us, but to God be the glory.

INTRODUCTION:

Welcome to Holy Yoga

*H*oly Yoga. Just the name tends to draw quizzical looks, raised eyebrows, and more than a few outright rejections. How can yoga be considered *holy*—in the Christian sense?

For something to be holy, it must be "dedicated or devoted to the service or worship of God, the church, or religion."[1] And that's exactly what this style of yoga is. It's not just any old yoga. It's not the yoga offered at your neighborhood studio or gym. It's not the yoga that relies on Hindu spirituality or teaches some form of oneness with the universe. This is *Holy Yoga,* and it's specifically for Christians and those who are seeking a relationship with Christ. The yoga I'm going to teach you is a profound physical worship of our Lord and Savior, Jesus Christ, through prayer, breath work, and movement.

I'm honored to have you with me. The Lord has given me a love and a passion for this practice of Holy Yoga that is almost hard for me to contain! He has inspired me to build a worldwide ministry that includes classes, teacher training, and audiovisual resources, and He has blessed the ministry with this book to help me share His glory with Christians and seekers everywhere.

Let me back up just a little bit and tell you how this all got started. I began practicing yoga in 1999 and have been teaching it since 2000. Back then, I was living life "in and of the world" and had not yet become a believer. But in the year 2001, everything changed. I was born again in our Lord Jesus Christ, and nothing has been the same since! One of the first things that changed for me was my practice of yoga. I immediately felt convicted to use my knowledge of yoga to worship and glorify the Lord. He began teaching me, step by step, how this was possible.

I started weaving the Word into my personal yoga practice. I found that as I set my intention to praise and glorify God, my yoga practice changed, taking on a new form that surpassed my previous experience and brought new levels of intensity. By inviting God to be part of this practice I was able to open myself to Him completely: physically, emotionally, and spiritually. I found my closeness to God, my ability to pray, and my understanding of my relationship with Him was deeply enhanced. When I shared this practice with others, it became collective worship, a prayer with the benefits of the physical principles of yoga.

I am not a theologian, a pastor, an elder, or even a seminary student. I have been re-created in the Lord and have a deep love and appreciation for His mercy and His grace. I believe that I am nurtured, restored, and replenished when I dedicate myself and my yoga practice to my Creator. I am speaking to you as a believer and a fellow pilgrim. I'm still learning—about Christ as well as about yoga. I hope we can be on this learning journey together.

What Is Holy Yoga?

The Holy Yoga experience is a time of worship, praise, and connection to Christ, practiced to contemporary Christian music. It teaches us to take time to love, nurture, accept, heal, and grow in His Word and in His Spirit.

Yoga is a physical exercise with the benefit of strengthening and improving flexibility of the muscles. But it is so much more. It is a practice designed to increase spiritual growth. Although yoga has become increasingly popular over the last few decades, few Christians know that it is also a unique way to worship God through the ancient practices and disciplines of body prayer. Christians can utilize the practice of yoga as a springboard to deeper levels of surrender and to focus their surrender in the presence of God. As a Christian and as a yoga practitioner, I founded Holy Yoga to create a place where the physical expression of yoga can be Christian worship.

Holy Yoga—or any form of Christian yoga—is not a religion. Rather, it is a practice of bodily alignment, mindful breathing, and purposeful reliance on God. Holy Yoga is dedicated to facilitating the worship and celebration of God through movement and meditation.

When led using Scripture, Holy Yoga is a practice that encourages patience and cultivates an understanding of what God can manifest in our bodies and emotions. When we distance ourselves from the daily grind and find peace in worshiping with the entirety of our beings, we find ourselves in the flow of His magnificence and in the midst of His grace.

Holy Yoga is all about Christ, all the time, so there's no need to be afraid! The Lord wants us to love and worship Him with our whole selves. In Mark 12:30 Jesus said, "Love the Lord your God with all your heart and with all your soul and with all your mind and with all your strength." That is our intention with Holy Yoga.

The Benefits of Holy Yoga

As a yoga student and teacher, I can really appreciate the health benefits of a mind/body connection as a means to a healthy lifestyle. But as a believer I know that God is the only authentic path to wellness. That is the great thing about this practice: Holy Yoga offers seekers and believers in Jesus Christ, regardless of denomination, an opportunity to bring together a healthy exterior and a sound spiritual interior.

Finding a practice that can simultaneously benefit the body, the mind, and the spirit is no easy task. Yet, that is exactly the essence of the countless benefits experienced by Holy Yoga practitioners.

At the physical level, the practice of yoga promotes all aspects of well-being through healing, strengthening, stretching, oxygenating, and relaxing the body. Some of the proven key benefits include improved muscle tone, better circulation, increased flexibility, strengthened joints, healthy weight maintenance, and pain management.

Through concentration, yoga promotes mental health as well. A clear and peaceful mind is alert and can more easily focus on the meaning and significance of Scripture. Yoga helps improve memory and concentration and can help alleviate symptoms of depression and mood swings. It promotes an overall sense of well-being because of the integration of mind, body, and spirit.

On the spiritual level, Holy Yoga practitioners can achieve a deeper relationship with the Lord. We worship and strengthen our bond with our Creator, allowing us to express prayer in a very intense yet intimate way. We dedicate our minds and bodies in prayer, increasing our reliance on God. It is a profound way to be closer to our Lord as we participate in a unique Christian worship.

Holy Yoga is right for you if you are seeking a relationship with God or are a Christian looking to combine the numerous and proven health benefits of a yoga practice with scriptural teachings and prayer.

But What About All Those Objections?

Believe me, I've heard all the objections, criticisms, and well-reasoned denunciations of Christian yoga. I'm sensitive and compassionate toward those whose consciences dictate a rejection of anything called "yoga." In chapter 4 we will look at many of the common doubts about Christian yoga. But I want to tell you right now I deeply believe that as we learn more about the practice of Christian yoga, we can embrace it as a completely holy discipline. As believers, we are called to follow God's leading, and He has strongly led me to the practice and teaching of Holy Yoga.

Some people have expressed a fear that the physical aspect of yoga can lead to a type of body worship. This is a valid concern rooted in historical occurrences, but it need not be a foregone conclusion. There are several other classical disciplines that are physical in nature, and when practiced properly, these do not lead us down the wrong path. Fasting is the most obvious example, but meditation, simplicity, solitude, and service are other disciplines that are all at least partly physical.

I've found that other people are concerned because yoga adherents claim that their goal is "union with God." Perhaps it is the word "union" that is troublesome. While traditional Eastern yoga looks at "union" as meaning "becoming one with God," Holy Yoga sees it as becoming surrendered to God, devoted to Him, and united with Him in purpose.

Let God Speak

If you have ever considered the powerful and proven benefits of practicing yoga but have been apprehensive about the intent, Holy Yoga is for you. It is an amazing opportunity to connect to God and glorify Him in your mind, body, and soul. This book will provide you clear links between Christian faith and the practice of yoga and meditation.

In the time we spend together I encourage you to really let go and let God move in and through you. In the intentional stillness of Holy Yoga, we can tune out of the worldly frequency that, even as believers, we become accustomed to and tune into God's frequency. Let God speak to you in that stillness of mind and unity with the Holy Spirit.

My prayer for you is that you embrace this with all the love and passion you have for the Lord, and to praise Him with everything you've got. I cannot imagine He would want it any other way!

Brooke Boon

PART ONE

Getting to Know Holy Yoga

CHAPTER I

Understanding Yoga

*May the God who gives endurance and encouragement give you a spirit of
unity among yourselves as you follow Christ Jesus.*
Romans 15:5

When I first began to practice yoga, I was attending secular
yoga classes that incorporated aspects of Eastern or
New Age thought. My teachers routinely encouraged their students
to "look within" to find their divinity. They whispered promptings
for us to seek enlightenment through oneness with the universe.
They taught that everything we need is all inside of us—we just
have to find it.

I guess it was intended to be a comforting and hopeful message.
But when I was told it was "all about me," I wasn't comforted at
all. Frankly, it scared me to death. I hadn't met Christ yet but I was
searching, and I knew that whatever I needed, it wasn't inside of
me. My train wreck of a life had given me clear evidence of that! I
would go to those classes and practice the postures, all the while
thinking that if it was really all about me, then I had a serious
problem. I didn't know much, but one thing was clear: I could not
continue to do life all by myself.

When I became a Christian and began learning how to use
yoga in my spiritual walk with Jesus, it was such a relief! How
comforting to know that living life in peace and joy doesn't depend

on *me*. Thank You, Jesus, for being my Savior, thank You that it's not all up to me!

I went into those secular classes unaware of the history, traditions, philosophies, and spiritual aspects of yoga. Like many Western practitioners of yoga today, I just wanted to get into shape! Being ignorant made me vulnerable to an Eastern spiritual influence, but praise God, it never became something that interested me. It actually never felt *right* to me. Once I was reborn in Jesus Christ, I finally knew why.

You don't need to know the entire history of yoga to understand what it is and how it can help you. I certainly don't want to bore you with a long history lesson. You can walk into a gym or yoga studio any day of the week and begin practicing yoga right away as I did, without knowing a thing. But there are certain things about yoga that are fascinating, and knowing them will help your practice and your motivation. There are also a few misunderstandings about yoga that we'll need to clear up, so that you're not going into this endeavor with false assumptions. Most importantly, there are distinctions that we'll need to make between Holy Yoga and all other styles.

First, let's get to know the basics about yoga.

What Is Yoga?

The whole system of yoga is built on three main structures: physical postures, breathing, and meditation. The postures (or poses) in yoga are designed to put pressure on the glandular systems of the body, thereby increasing the body's efficiency and total health. The muscles are alternately stretched and contracted, and spaces are made in the joints to increase elasticity and range of motion. Yoga looks upon the body as the primary instrument that enables us to work and evolve in the world, and so a yoga student treats it with great care and respect.

Breathing techniques are based on the concept that breath is the source of life in the body. The yoga student gently increases breath control to improve the health and function of both body and mind. These two systems of poses and breathing then prepare the body and mind for meditation, and the student finds an easy approach to a quiet mind that allows silence and healing from everyday stress. Regular daily practice of all three parts of this structure of yoga produce a clear, bright mind and a strong, capable body.

No one knows exactly when yoga began, but it certainly predates written history. Stone carvings depicting figures in yoga positions have been found in archeological sites in the Indus Valley dating back five thousand years or more.[1] There is a common misconception that yoga is rooted in Hinduism; on the contrary, Hinduism's religious structures evolved much later and incorporated some of the physical practices of yoga. Other religions throughout the world have also incorporated physical practices and ideas related to yoga.

The tradition of yoga has always been passed on individually from teacher to student through oral instruction and practical demonstration. The formal techniques that are now known as yoga are, therefore, based on the collective experiences of many individuals over centuries. The particular manner in which the techniques are taught and practiced today depends on the approach passed down in the line of teachers supporting the individual practitioner.

The word *yoga* comes from an ancient Sanskrit word meaning "unity" or "to join." It also connotes discipline or effort. Yoga is about using discipline and effort toward the goal of unity.[2]

Scripture has much to say about unity! Jesus prayed for His disciples and all believers that we would be unified in each other and in Him (John 17:20–24). The apostle Paul urged us repeatedly to be unified in the body of Christ. In Colossians 3:14, Paul reminded us that love is the virtue that "binds them all together in perfect unity."

But is the unity of yoga the same as the unity we pursue as Christians? Traditionally, yoga is the discipline of unifying the body, mind, and spirit. In Holy Yoga, we pursue unity of body, mind, and His Holy Spirit that dwells within us, *with the intent of worshiping and serving Christ with our entire beings.*

Many of us walk around in a fragmented state, whether or not we realize it. We experience our emotions separate from our thoughts; we experience our bodies as distinct from our minds; we disconnect our spiritual lives from everything else, relating to God only on Sunday mornings or in dedicated times of prayer. In truth, all this compartmentalization is a false way of living. We are integrated beings: our thoughts, feelings, bodily experiences, and spiritual longings are all a part of who we are and are not meant to be experienced as separate.

In order to worship God fully and to experience the lives He has set out for us, we need to be our most authentic, real, whole selves. Holy Yoga is a means to unifying ourselves so that we can open up fully to God's grace and love. Think about how this might play out in your life. You may be mentally willing and seeking the Lord, but your emotions are a mess. Or perhaps you are seeking God with your heart, but your mind can't seem to grasp the reality. You might be desiring closeness with the Lord, but your body is betraying you in some way, through pain or illness, and it causes you to falter on your spiritual path. All these schisms between mind, body, and spirit prevent us from experiencing the fullness of God, which then diminishes our ability to worship Him completely.

As we work to unify our bodies, minds, and spirits with the Lord, we also naturally open up to more genuine union with others around us. This leads directly to one of the goals of our Christian lives: to be "one in the Spirit," or unified in the body of Christ. I like the way Paul put it in his letter to the Ephesians: "Make every effort to keep the unity of the Spirit through the bond of peace. There is one body and one Spirit—just as you were called to one hope when you were called—one Lord, one faith, one baptism; one God and Father of all, who is over all and through all and in all" (4:3–6). The idea of unity is a beautiful, biblical picture of God's perfect desire for His people.

Classical Yoga Theories

A scholar named Patanjali compiled one of the earliest texts having to do with yoga. He set down the most prevalent yoga theories and practices of his time in a book he called *Yoga Sutras,* translated "Yoga Aphorisms" (an aphorism is a concise statement of a principle). Patanjali wrote somewhere between the first century BC and the fifth century AD. The system he wrote about is generally referred to today as Classical Yoga.

The eight steps of Classical Yoga are:

1) restraint—refraining from violence, lying, stealing, casual sex, and hoarding.
2) observance—purity, contentment, tolerance, study, and remembrance.
3) physical exercises.
4) breathing techniques.
5) preparation for meditation.
6) concentration—being able to hold the mind on one object for a specified time.
7) meditation—the ability to focus on one thing (or nothing) indefinitely.
8) absorption—the realization of the essential nature of the self.

Yoga probably arrived in the United States in the late 1800s, but it did not become widely known until the 1960s. As more became known about the beneficial effects of yoga, it gained acceptance and respect as a valuable method for helping in the management of stress and improving health and well-being. Many physicians now recommend yoga practice to patients at risk for heart disease, as well as those with back pain, arthritis, depression, and other chronic conditions. (Always check with your doctor before beginning any exercise program.)

Yoga is a system of techniques that can be used for a number of goals, from simply managing stress better, learning to relax, and increasing flexibility all the way to becoming more self-aware and acquiring the deepest knowledge of one's own self in Christ. I have developed Holy Yoga specifically for the purpose of increasing health—mind, body, and spirit—while consciously seeking a deeper relationship with the Lord Jesus Christ.

The type of yoga most of us are familiar with involves stretching our bodies into various postures. This is the physical element and is known as *Hatha* Yoga. Hatha Yoga also incorporates mindful breathing, relaxation, and meditation. It is the yoga of physical discipline. Holy Yoga is also based on Bhakti Yoga, the yoga of devotion. Its goal is to connect or even merge with a supreme being through acts of devotion. Our *Bhakti* Yoga is all about getting in touch with the Holy Spirit by following the outpourings of our hearts, although we certainly don't have "merging with" the Holy Spirit as our goal, since we know that's impossible as well as a heretical idea. The term *bhakti* can be roughly translated to mean "devotion," and this, coupled with the Christian concept of faith, leads to a state of mind that can be described as *being immersed in the Holy Spirit.* This strand of yoga principally advocates love and devotion.

Our use of the postures of Hatha Yoga together with the spiritual intent—although thoroughly Christian—of Bhakti Yoga are what make our practice of yoga truly *holy*.

Yoga as a Philosophy

Yoga can be thought of as a philosophy. It's the idea that by bringing a union of focus between mind and body, while simultaneously making the mind and body stronger and more flexible, we become more authentic people, able to hear God and experience Him in previously impossible ways. While other religions have used this philosophy to meet their own requirements, such as looking for God inside oneself or seeking oneness with the environment, the Holy Yoga approach is to seek Christ only. We were created to have a relationship with our heavenly Father, so the focus is on Christ, the goal is Christ, and the result is a deeper relationship with and experience of Him.

The central doctrine of ancient, traditional yoga philosophy is that nothing exists beyond the mind and its consciousness, which is the only ultimate reality. As practitioners of Holy Yoga, we recognize this original idea but reject it in favor of biblical truth. Ancient yoga's goal was to bring participants to the "ultimate truth." Our goal in Holy Yoga is the same—it's just that we have a different definition of "truth." We know that Jesus is "the way and the truth and the life" and that no one gets to the Father except through Him (John 14:6). We seek only the truth of Jesus Christ.

Yoga as Art and Science

Besides being a philosophy, yoga is also a little bit science and a little bit art. The science behind it confirms that the practice of stretching the body—opening up spaces in joints, loosening muscles, and purposefully relaxing—is a major benefit to good health. There are so many physical benefits that for some people, yoga's effects seem nothing short of miraculous. Perhaps yoga's primary advantage in our busy lives today is its effectiveness in stress management. Chapter 6 explores in detail the proven health benefits.

The art of yoga comes in the numerous, individualized ways we practice. There are specific postures, techniques, and attitudes that are part of the package. But we all practice in our own ways, according to our unique bodies, minds, and spiritual experiences. It is an art much like dancing. While the steps may be choreographed, it is the individual dancer who breathes life into the form, making it a beautiful expression full of feeling and depth. Practicing yoga can be quite fulfilling for the "artist" in each of us.

Holy Yoga embraces the physical, mental, emotional, and spiritual realms, with the focus always on opening up to God and connecting with Him. Holy Yoga is all about Jesus and learning to depend on Him more and more fully as our spiritual growth progresses.

Styles of American Yoga

Yoga has been practiced in the West for only about the last century. Since Americans began embracing yoga, several new "styles" or brands of yoga have been developed by various teachers to better meet the needs of Westerners.

It can be confusing if you look in the phone book or drive down the street and see names like "Ashtanga Yoga" or "Bikram Yoga" or "Kripalu Yoga." The names are simply telling you what style that studio teaches. One style may focus more on bodily alignment, while another focuses on athletic "power"-type moves. Some styles emphasize the individual's needs and capacity, while others encourage precise implementation of each posture regardless of unique body types.

Each style was originated by a particular yoga teacher and has been carried on by other teachers and students over time. Since there are hundreds of books, articles, and Web sites available to explain the various styles of yoga, I'm not going to describe them in detail, but feel free to consult other sources if you would like to learn more.

All these styles of yoga involve the traditional yoga postures that teachers have been passing down through generations for thousands of years. The postures themselves are similar no matter where you go—anywhere in the world! But the sequence of postures, the manner in which they're undertaken, and the mental/spiritual intent vary. How does Holy Yoga fit into this picture? Holy Yoga has been developed to be yet another unique "style" of yoga. We use the same basic body positions as in all of yoga. But we use them in conjunction with specific language to help accentuate the physical pose and to worship God, connect with Christ, and be filled with the Spirit.

The idea of Christian yoga isn't brand-new. Thomas Ryan, a Catholic priest and scholar, has studied yoga in depth for many years. His 1995 book, *Prayer of Heart and Body,* was an important work establishing yoga as legitimate Christian discipline. His more recent work, *Reclaiming the Body in Christian Spirituality,* takes the idea further by examining the role of the body in Christian spiritual life. He encourages a healthy spiritual attitude toward our bodies and shows us how our physical activities are acts of worship toward our Creator, God.

More recently, Episcopal priest Nancy Roth has been studying and teaching yoga and has authored a wonderful little book, *An Invitation to Christian Yoga.* Some of her teachings, though seemingly simple, have been life-changing for me as I came to understand the profound spirituality inherent in the movement of the body in union with the mind and spirit.

Why Is Yoga So Popular?

Larry Payne, coauthor of *Yoga for Dummies* and *Yoga Rx,* calls yoga a "natural, do-it-yourself prescription for good health and stress management."[3] Sounds great, doesn't it? I think that definition embodies the reason for the popularity of yoga.

Today we know that stress is one of the greatest contributors to poor health. Stress makes a healthy body more open to disease and worsens the effects of most illnesses and ailments. On top of all that, being stressed just doesn't feel good! Yoga is one of the best ways to calm a stressed mind and body.

But people have many different reasons for wanting to do yoga. The most important motive for Americans is to "stay in shape." This can mean losing or maintaining weight, increasing muscle tone and flexibility, or simply staying physically fit. Yoga can accomplish all of these goals, but the purely physical effects were never the intent of yoga. If you enter a local yoga studio with entirely physical goals and are unaware of the spiritual content that particular class comprises, you can possibly find yourself spiritually compromised. This will never happen with Holy Yoga! Even if you approach Holy Yoga with a physical motivation, you'll find it safe for your Christian walk.

Another reason some people practice yoga is for specifically therapeutic purposes. More than just a general "staying in shape," these practitioners are seeking relief from specific illnesses or bodily ailments. Yoga therapy has been developed to address all manner of problems, including chronic back pain, asthma, heart disease, arthritis, and chronic fatigue syndrome. In fact, yoga has proven so effective in managing some chronic diseases and pain issues that some insurance companies offer coverage for yoga therapy.[4] Because of its proven effectiveness in relieving or managing all types of physical problems, yoga has continued to increase in popularity even as other disciplines such as Pilates and tai chi have also become popular.

Many people practice yoga as a spiritual discipline, which is our central focus in Holy Yoga. But the idea of yoga as a Christian spiritual discipline is still not very widespread, so we are always careful to distinguish Christ-centered yoga from all the other types. The idea of seeking *enlightenment* is common in yoga circles. We need to be clear in delineating this idea from what we are taught in Scripture. While enlightenment traditionally refers to a deep experience of the core of *the self,* as Christians we are seeking communion with Christ. This does, of course, entail a more profound knowledge of the self. But self-awareness is not our final goal—Christ-awareness is.

One of my students, Peggy, said, "Holy Yoga is a special time for me to worship God fully with mind and body." That's the whole idea behind the practice of Holy Yoga! Before you go any farther in your exploration of yoga as a Christian practice, take some time to ask yourself: *Why do I want to do yoga? What's my goal?*

Set your intention first. Focus your goal on God and whatever He wants for you. Dedicate your practice to Him and Him alone. Only then will Holy Yoga become your own unique way to worship God with all of yourself through the ancient disciplines of bodily prayer.

CHAPTER 2

The Holiness of Yoga

Wait for the LORD; be strong and take heart and wait for the LORD.
Psalm 27:14

One of my students tells this story:

After several years of deep connection with God, a daily prayer life, and joyful service through my church, I hit a roadblock in my faith journey. I became disenchanted with organized religion and got angry about the exclusivity and judgment I perceived. I disengaged from the church—and my faith.

For the next few years, my family attended church sporadically but I remained distant from service and involvement. I intended to continue my prayer life on my own and not let my personal relationship with God suffer because of what was going on at the church. But it was harder than I thought, and I slowly slipped away from daily prayer, many of my Christian friends, and my joyful, Christ-centered life.

Then one day while at a yoga class at the YMCA, I overheard a woman in the class talking about her new Holy Yoga outreach—a yoga ministry she was just beginning to get off the ground. Though I didn't know Brooke at the time, her passion for yoga and God overflowed as she described her vision. I thought about that conversation for a long time.

Eventually I decided to try Brooke's Holy Yoga class at a local church. I never expected it to change my life! Since starting my Holy Yoga practice, I've begun to open my mind and body to Christ again. And in the opening postures of Holy Yoga, I've found Christ's open arms welcoming me back. I've experienced the loving-kindness that Christ taught—and I've begun to meditate, use scriptural meditations, and pray again. Holy Yoga nudged me back to Christ—with music, movement, meditation, and love. I've found an opening to my faith, and I am happy to slip in the back door!

With such wonderful testimonies, it seems strange that we Westerners took so long to discover and embrace the powerful practice of yoga. But it makes sense in the larger context of the huge cultural and religious differences between Eastern and Western civilizations. It has been only in the last couple of centuries, and particularly the last few decades, that the world has become "smaller" and cultures have more readily mingled and borrowed traditions from one another.

In today's culture, Christians of different denominations are opening up to worship styles from other traditions. Many believers are newly interested in traditional spiritual disciplines such as meditation, fasting, solitude, and simplicity. Ancient rituals such as prayer labyrinths, in which Christians pray to and praise God while enacting a metaphorical journey to Him, are becoming more widely utilized as a way to meditate on God's glory and grace. Christians are learning how to pray and seek God in other ways besides kneeling at their bedsides and bowing their heads. I've noticed many people growing their faith from a visit on Sunday to an intimate daily relationship. The Vatican has even recognized that Christians are opening up to various body postures as a way to facilitate prayer.[1] Our culture is finally at the point of being able to adopt a discipline such as yoga into the Christian lexicon.

Yoga as Christian Discipline

In his classic book *Celebration of Discipline,* Richard Foster reminds us that "the classical Disciplines of the spiritual life call us to move beyond surface living into the depths."[2] While yoga cannot be considered a "classical" Christian discipline, it nevertheless has the same goal and can have similar effects as other disciplines, provided it is practiced with the right intent. It can take us into the depths of a relationship with Christ.

Having an appropriate *purpose* in the practice of a discipline is what makes it holy or not. Like many disciplines, yoga can be practiced by two people using the exact same physical moves, with one coming into closer communion with God and the other not. It depends upon the intent, as do all disciplines. Compare it to the classical discipline of fasting. You can undertake a spiritual fast, spending time in prayer and meditation and worship. Your fast will be holy. It is about God. On the other hand, plenty of atheists fast frequently. Their purpose is not spiritual but physical, having to do with their bodily health and cleansing. Their fasts are not holy. It's the same with our practice of yoga: we make the discipline holy by placing our intent squarely on Christ.

If we're looking at Holy Yoga as a discipline, what then is its purpose? Foster tells us, "The disciplines are God's way of getting us into the ground; they put us where He can work within us and transform us. By themselves the Spiritual Disciplines can do nothing; they can only get us to the place where something can be done."[3] I couldn't have come up with a better explanation for Holy Yoga! It is a discipline because it is a gift of God, a means of His grace, and a place we go to be in a position for Him to work in and through us.

As Jerry Bridges points out in his book *The Pursuit of Holiness,* "It is possible to establish convictions regarding a life of holiness, and even make a definite commitment to that end, yet fail to achieve the goal." He goes on to explain that the only way to obtain godliness is through discipline. While most of us are aware of that fact, we also tend to find it suspect. We prefer to focus on our freedom in Christ! We try, at all costs, to avoid "legalism."[4]

Yet the apostle Paul put it clearly when he wrote, "Train yourself to be godly" (1 Tim. 4:7). He encouraged us with a reminder that God gave us a spirit of self-discipline (2 Tim. 1:7). I've found that Holy Yoga is one of the most powerful ways to discipline myself— my mind, spirit, and body—toward godliness. Especially when practiced in conjunction with the classical spiritual disciplines, Holy Yoga is a profound tool for Christian spiritual development.

Yoga Helps Christians Pray

The most commonly practiced discipline in Christian life is, of course, prayer. As I've studied and read numerous books on prayer, I've been fascinated to discover that all of the most distinguished and revered Christians in history have struggled with it! Every classic writer from Saint Augustine to Brother Lawrence to C. S. Lewis has written about his effort to concentrate and remain focused in prayer. Even Jesus' closest disciples, Peter, James, and John, in their moment of weakness fell asleep in the Garden of Gethsemane while they were supposed to be praying (Mark 14:32–42).

Frederica Mathewes-Green wrote, "Most of the time, even at worship, our minds are jumbled with a thousand other things. Throughout the ancient liturgy are regular reminders to pay attention. 'Let us stand upright! Let us stand with fear! Let us attend!' the deacon is instructed to say, and often he's saying it to himself as much as to anyone else."[5] Isn't it comforting to know that we're not the only ones striving, often unsuccessfully, to have a focused prayer life?

This is where Holy Yoga finds its deepest and most powerful purpose. In order for us to be attentive to God, we need to quiet the mind and the body of all worldly distractions—a nearly impossible feat in today's noisy environment! Yoga's techniques are aimed at this goal. Even novice Holy Yoga practitioners find their openness and responsiveness to God intensifies immediately as they discipline their bodies and minds toward quietness.

To better appreciate how Holy Yoga helps us pray, it's helpful to consider the reasons we pray in the first place. First, we pray because God has made it clear in Scripture that it's our responsibility and our primary means of relating to Him. Prayer is one of the most important ways we seek His kingdom (Matt. 6:33). We pray because we are dependent beings—not by any means the autonomous creatures we imagine ourselves. We have needs and desires that we cannot meet on our own, and so by prayer we present our petitions and requests before God (Phil. 4:6). However, the essence of prayer lies not in our fervent requests, but in our growing relationship with the Lord. In other words, it's not the end result that counts—it's the journey.

Hank Hanegraaff helps us grasp this truth through a contemporary analogy: "For Tiger [Woods], playing golf is its own reward. It is obvious that he loves the *process* more than he loves the *prize*. For Christians, prayer should be its own reward. Prayer is not a magic formula to get things from God. Communing with God in prayer is itself the prize."[6]

This is so important as it relates to Holy Yoga. As with prayer, the essence is in the process, not the result. And amazingly, Holy Yoga facilitates our pursuing prayer as "itself the prize" by teaching us to let go of all those noisy words we tend to throw at God and simply *be* in His presence.

The depth of communion with God that Holy Yoga can bring about has led me to my own saying: "I pray, therefore I am." I am reminded that without God, *I am not!* Whenever I hear the oft-repeated Descartes quote, "I think, therefore I am," it feels so worldly and self-focused. I know the statement expresses a complex philosophy, but my surface reaction is, *I did not think myself into existence! I was created by God and I am sustained, every moment of every day, by the very breath of God.* "Every good and perfect gift is from above, coming down from the Father" (James 1:17). It is only by continually seeking Him that we are able to receive His gifts—the gift of Himself the most precious of all.

Holy Yoga helps us pray by teaching us to cultivate a quiet heart and mind. As Thomas Ryan put it, "It invites cerebral Western world people to 'get out of their heads.'"[7] This is crucial in helping us master one of the most important yet neglected aspects of prayer—listening. We cannot hear God speaking to our hearts if our minds are cluttered with requests, worries, and complaints.

Holy Yoga does more than simply assist us in our prayer lives. In addition to reinforcing what is prayed, physical prayer *becomes prayer itself.*[8] The movement of our bodies, and the appreciation of God's gift to us of these holy vessels, allows us to worship our Creator not just through our thoughts and our words, but through the very physical entities in which we live.

Practicing Yoga as Prayer

When I'm teaching a Holy Yoga class, I often tell my students, "We could all use a checkup from the neck up!" This is all about getting our hearts and our heads on the same page. By opening up to God through the practice of yoga, I often feel in my heart what God is saying to me before I "know" it in my head. We take time to feel, to experience, and to listen to God, away from the noise of the world, to give our hearts and minds a chance to connect.

In the world we are constantly inundated with information. We exist in a perpetual state of sensory overload. We have so much knowledge, so many facts that in some ways we each bear the weight of the world on our shoulders every day. We attach meaning to things that are meaningless, and we often miss the profound truths that are right before our eyes.

In Holy Yoga we seek to step aside from the drama and the racket and give our hearts and heads a chance to get at the truth. I like to tell my students, "This is a time-out from the world and a time-in with God." You can look at your own Holy Yoga practice the same way, creating a quiet space and time specifically to worship with your mind, body, and soul. Holy Yoga facilitates authentic prayer by teaching us to clear away the clutter in our bodies, minds, and spirits. We de-stress our bodies and wring out the negative tensions, elevating our physical and spiritual energy so that we can achieve a genuine connection with Him.

Sometimes when attending church or participating in Bible study, I am reminded that we tend to put God in a box. We think of Him almost like a genie in a bottle, listening to our wishes and capriciously deciding which ones to grant; judging one moment, bestowing grace the next. But we all know that God is so much bigger and more expansive than we can ever possibly comprehend! Holy Yoga is about removing the barriers little by little, seeking to *know* Him rather than to know *about* Him, and to experience Him as fully as possible.

A student and teacher of Holy Yoga, Kristy, put it this way:

> Holy Yoga is about balance for me between the gentle and energetic. The gentle classes allow me to take the time to be more reflective, pray, and listen to His will for me. Energetic classes are more of a time of praise and worship where I express my complete affection for the Lord through biblical meditation and movement. I love it! It is an amazing addition to the cultivation of my relationship with my heavenly Father.

Kristy's experience reflects one of the greatest aspects of Holy Yoga, the fact that it integrates our whole selves—heart, soul, mind, and strength. We'll look more deeply at that in the next chapter.

CHAPTER 3

Worshiping God with Our Whole Selves

Love the Lord your God with all your heart and with all your soul
and with all your mind and with all your strength.
Mark 12:30

*I*sn't it funny that the Lord's greatest commandment is one that otherwise devoted Christians often minimize or brush off? In Mark 12:30, Jesus declared that He wants us to love God with every aspect of our beings: heart, soul, mind, and strength. We rarely take the time to comprehend exactly what this means. Instead we tend to simplify it in our minds: *God wants us to love Him with everything we've got.* But let's stop generalizing for a moment and consider what the greatest commandment is really calling us to do.

I love Eugene Peterson's paraphrase of Mark 12:30 in The Message: "So love the Lord God with all your passion and prayer and intelligence and energy." That gets us closer to grasping the full extent of God's direction. I am to pursue God not just using every facet of who I am but *these specific* parts of me.

It's a little easier for me to begin visualizing this idea when I think of the various ways different Christian traditions have approached seeking and worshiping God. Some Christian traditions emphasize the intellectual aspects of the faith, seeking God through head knowledge of the Bible and its teachings. Others embrace the emotions as the primary tool for spiritual connection, as when you are singing worship songs and are overcome with a profound feeling of connection and spirituality. Still others accentuate our free will and our ability to make decisions, those moments when the Word of God convicts us and leads us to change something in our lives. Some traditions embrace our physical selves by raising hands in worship, clapping, or dancing. Take a moment to consider the ways in which *you* have sought to love and worship the Lord. Have you engaged your passion, prayer, intelligence, and energy? If you're like most people, chances are you've emphasized one or two of these aspects over the others.

Heart, Soul, Mind, and Strength Defined

Since the idea of heart-soul-mind-strength is so important, I am going to attempt to briefly describe each one here. Please know that these are not deep or definitive descriptions, but a quick summary of my understanding of what each one means. The definitions are partly based on the explanations given in Bob Rognlien's *Experiential Worship*.[1]

Heart

The thing He gave us in which we could experience His fullness and grace in love. Biblical uses of the word "heart" point us to our human will or *intention,* the power to make decisions for ourselves. The heart also refers to the deepest part of our human existence and experience.

Soul

The thing He longs to connect to, to fill, guide, sustain, nurture. Soul usually refers to the *emotional* aspects of being human, and along with the heart, also points to the deeper aspects of self.

Mind

The gift of our ability to process information, to make sense of it and to gain wisdom. He allows us to be in partial control of our minds, to choose whether we use them toward his glory.

Strength

The bodies He gave us, that His glory would be revealed in and through us. Strength usually refers to our physical being.

Holy Yoga's goal is to teach us to bring these four points of focus together simultaneously. We practice yoga with the *intention* of glorifying Him. We allow our *emotions* to surface so that we can offer them up to God. We empty our *minds* of clutter and fill them with nothing but Him. And we increase the health and *strength* of our physical bodies, offering Him gratitude and praise for this great gift.

A note before we move on: these four aspects of our selves are not separate and distinct, but rather fully integrated. We talk about them separately for ease of understanding, but we can't let that deceive us into thinking that these four descriptors actually describe distinct parts of ourselves. We cannot disconnect them. They are not puzzle pieces that fit together and can be taken apart; rather, they are like the ingredients of a cake: the flour, water, sugar, eggs, and oil are definitely in there. But once the batter is mixed up and the cake is baked, it's no longer possible to separate or distinguish those ingredients. That's the true nature of our heart, soul, mind, and strength.[2]

As I thought about this, I realized that each aspect of our selves also has the potential to be a major stumbling block in our lives. Sin can come from our thoughts, our emotions, our decisions, or our bodies. No wonder Jesus took the time to delineate heart-soul-mind-strength. He wants us to intentionally dedicate each aspect of ourselves to loving the Lord our God, thus helping us to avoid stumbling.

Body Prayer

Modern-day Christians are able to accept the heart-soul-mind thing, but the body? We don't often think about ways we can worship the Lord with our physical presence. How easily we accept some portions of God's Word and disregard others! I've found that Christians today have a hard time with the idea of "praying with their bodies." Many have been steeped in a tradition that teaches prayer, by definition, as "words." We might accept that those words swell from our hearts and minds and souls. But how can a prayer be from the body?

When the disciples asked Jesus to teach them to pray, He gave them a pattern of words to use when approaching the Father. I think this is where we sometimes get stuck in thinking that prayer can *only* be words. But consider 1 Corinthians 6:20: "You were bought at a price. Therefore honor God with your body." Or listen to Paul's impassioned plea to the Romans: "Therefore, I urge you, brothers, in view of God's mercy, to offer your bodies as living sacrifices, holy and pleasing to God—this is your spiritual act of worship" (Rom. 12:1). These verses and others like them speak to me of the body's important role in our spirituality, especially in the love and worship of our Lord.

I am going to talk about the physical aspect of loving our Lord more than the others because it's the part that most Christians seem to have trouble with, and because yoga is outwardly a physical discipline that ultimately involves the heart, soul, and mind as well. Again, even as we are discussing the body's role in prayer and worship, let's keep in mind that the body is not separable from the other aspects of ourselves.

As twenty-first-century Westerners, we are oriented toward the intellect. The fact that I'm writing this, and you're reading these words on paper, is an example of the way we approach things from the head first. In fact, there is a limit to what I can explain to you about the ways we worship and pray with our physical selves. After you've read all my words, you still won't get it. That's because Holy Yoga is an experience. It's a discipline, and like all disciplines, it defies complete explanation. It must be *experienced* to be understood, and even after you've encountered it and you have a gut-level comprehension of it, you'll probably find that you still cannot adequately convey it with words. It's like our faith. We will never fully comprehend intellectually the intricacy and vastness of God, but we are called to *believe*.

In our Western culture, we tend to think of physicality and spirituality as opposite and incompatible, an idea hammered into modern thought by the Enlightenment. A few Christian denominations embrace a worldview that doesn't disconnect the mind and body, such as the Pentecostals, who generally are not afraid to lift their arms, clap, and even dance as part of worship.[3] But that's as far as the acceptance of the body in worship usually goes.

Nancy Roth observes that many Christians throughout the ages had the habit of "denying or subduing the body, rather than welcoming the body as a partner and companion in prayer."[4] It is true that superstition, idolatry, blasphemy, and body worship can result from purely physical expressions of spirituality, as has happened in the past. But we cannot turn away from Jesus's instruction to include our "strength" in loving God. We have to find ways to use our bodies as part of our overall intent to connect with God.

While we don't often see it, Scripture is chock-full of references to God's positive view of the material realm. Pastor Bob Rognlien asserts in *Experiential Worship* that "the Bible offers an unwavering affirmation of the goodness of the physical order and its direct connection to spiritual realities."[5] The Bible opens with God creating the physical—the earth and everything in it, including the first man. He called it "very good." The Bible ends with the promise of a "new earth" (Rev. 21:1)—not an ethereal, spiritual dimension but a solid creation.

The two most crucial doctrines of Christianity, the Incarnation and the Resurrection, both comprise the sacredness of the physical. John 1:14 tells us, "The Word became flesh and made his dwelling among us." God's greatest gift to us, His Son, appeared in the physical body of a man. And as much as Christ's earthly ministry was about teaching people spiritual truths, it was largely accomplished through physical means: restoring a blind man's sight by rubbing his eyes with dirt and His own spittle, washing the disciples' feet, writing mysterious words in the dust with His finger, healing a soldier's severed ear with a touch, and subjecting Himself to the utmost suffering and pain in the Crucifixion. The Resurrection was about Jesus' conquering death and reappearing in a real, tangible body, further emphasizing the importance of the material realm that God created.

I am so touched by the words Jesus spoke to the disciples at the Last Supper, when He gave instructions for what we call the Eucharist or Holy Communion: "And he took bread, gave thanks and broke it, and gave it to them, saying, 'This is my body given for you; do this in remembrance of me'" (Luke 22:19). This speaks to me of the incredible interconnectedness of body and spirit, and the deep sacredness of the physical vessels in which we live. He gave His very body for us—we dare not diminish the magnitude of that.

God created all physical matter, so there is no justification for us to denigrate it, although we must always be careful not to elevate the body and material things above their proper place. Consider Paul's words: "Do you not know that your body is a temple of the Holy Spirit, who is in you, whom you have received from God?" (1 Cor. 6:19). We're familiar with this metaphor of our bodies as temples. How often have we tried to get below the surface of what that means? Surely it tells us that as "houses" for God, we should not defile ourselves or treat our bodies as other than holy. But what, exactly, is a temple?

In today's language, we would think of a temple as a church. It is not only metaphorically *where God lives,* but tangibly, a church is a place within which we worship the Lord. So our bodies are places *within which we worship the Lord.* That is why I've developed Holy Yoga—so that we can have a means of worshiping the Lord in our bodies, as an entryway to worshiping with our hearts, souls, and minds.

Lauren Winner wrote, "Christianity has the words to offer a spirituality of the body, but the church hasn't always spoken those words."[6] While Christians recognize all the ways Scripture points to the sacredness of the physical, we have not tended to place our focus there in the modern-day church. We certainly don't speak of it much. Yet, Christians have always lived a faith of the body.[7]

Without thinking, we kneel, bow our heads, or fold our hands to pray. We stand up to praise the Lord while using our vocal cords to sing. Some of us even raise our arms! We take Communion, we make the sign of the cross, we walk a prayer labyrinth, we participate in a fast. These are ordinary actions abounding with divine significance. The fact is that we use our bodies in some fashion no matter what we are doing. We can ignore the significance of our bodies, but that seems to me a waste of a precious resource! The way we use our bodies in worship will "either help or hinder our experience of God."[8] Why not use them intentionally as instruments of prayer and praise?

Holy Yoga is powerful because it fully engages the body, and the body is intricately tied to all the other parts of our selves. Yoga is known to provide a profound feeling of physical well-being, sometimes even experienced as joy. As "unspiritual" as it may sound, when we are experiencing deep pleasure we are much closer to being able to have a recognizable experience of holiness. The body is a powerful ally in the quest to draw closer to God.[9]

The Mystery of It All

In this age of science, we are so accustomed to being able to understand how things work that we tend to reject or shy away from anything that seems mysterious or incomprehensible. Yet so much of God is mystery, existing outside of anything we can understand. People throughout history have devised ways to delve into that mystery, to try to experience it even if they could not grasp it. Instinctually, people have always known that there are ways to experience God that defy logic and reason.

We value our minds above all else. If we can think it and know it intellectually, then it must exist. But we have to remind ourselves that God exists far outside this capacity to think. That's why disciplines such as prayer, fasting, and meditation have been developed over the centuries by devoted Christ-followers. They take us beyond what we can think into a realm of experience that is of the heart and body and soul. These disciplines draw us closer to God through means that are more mysterious than simply reading the Bible or praying.

Even ancient liturgies have a major element of mystery to them. We might read The Book of Common Prayer and think, *This is just a lot of repetition of Bible verses*. But it's so much more. The repetition is another means of clearing the mind of distractions, calming the body, and attempting a complete heart-mind-body connection to God.

One of my students, Michelle, says: "By fully integrating the physical and spiritual aspects of my being during Holy Yoga, the integration of the emotional and intellectual aspects of my being comes more naturally in the rest of my life." Yes, it's a mystery how this works. Part of the practice of yoga depends upon acceptance of these great mysteries. How can body movement be prayer? It cannot be explained in words on paper. But we don't have to understand it to make use of our bodies and appreciate them as the gifts they are and employ them in the full love and worship of our Lord and Savior, Jesus Christ.

CHAPTER 4

Answering the Objections

We are not trying to please men but God, who tests our hearts.
1 Thessalonians 2:4

A couple of years ago when I was beginning my Holy Yoga Ministries, a man called on the phone asking to talk to me about "Christian yoga." I'll call him Richard, though it is not his real name. Richard had a ministry for which he wanted to interview me.

I prayed about the opportunity and sought wise counsel. I was advised not to do the interview, simply because my own ministry was still in its infancy and I was not yet prepared to fully explain it to people for whom the idea of "Christian yoga" would seem oxymoronic. I still wasn't sure, so I left the question in the hands of God. Before I felt I had an answer directly from Him, Richard phoned me back and cancelled the interview. I guess I got my answer!

Later, through a complex series of events, I found out that Richard was quite critical of Holy Yoga, and that people who followed his ministry had also expressed malicious disapproval of the concept that yoga could be Christian.

While I believe Richard is sincere in his efforts to bring the truth of Christ to people, and I understand the truths from which the fears and doubts about yoga spring, I also feel sad that so many people make judgments without taking the time to delve deep into the subject at hand. I ended up having a further conversation with Richard in which he told me, "There is no such thing as 'holy yoga.'" I responded by politely disagreeing, saying that I did not understand exactly what he meant, because in fact *holy yoga* was a large part of my reality.

Richard responded, "That's because *your reality is Satanic*."

I realize that this may be the earnestly held perspective of many Christians whose hearts are dedicated to Him and who genuinely desire to serve the Lord. But my own experience has taught me that this view is not the truth. I hope that the preceding three chapters have shown you that my heart, my practice of yoga, and my life are dedicated to the one and only Almighty God, Creator of heaven and earth. But I also want to talk about the deep and abiding Christian objections to yoga and discuss how they do not apply to Holy Yoga.

We've already discussed the fact that Holy Yoga is completely about connection with Christ. But I don't want to minimize or ignore the fact that spiritual compromise *is possible* if you enter a yoga class that is not Christ-centered. As I go through the various oppositions to Holy Yoga, I hope to convey an appreciation for the origin of each of the arguments. Each of the concerns is rooted in the truth of Scripture and may well apply to traditional Eastern yoga, yet because of the uniqueness of Christ-centered yoga, these concerns are not applicable here.

The bottom line is that we can debate all day long about yoga's roots, its history, and all the other ways that the world uses it. But the conversation would be irrelevant because in Holy Yoga, our entire intent and focus are completely on Jesus Christ. There is simply no room in our practice for anything else.

Nevertheless, if you're a Christian and decide to practice Holy Yoga, you may be subjected to criticism or at the very least, questioning. Because your Christian witness is important, and because I want you to be confident that it really is okay to practice yoga as a Christian discipline, I'm going to give you straight answers to the most common criticisms I've heard.

The usual criticisms of yoga from a Christian standpoint fall into a few major categories:

- "Yoga can't be separated from the Hindu religion."
- "Yoga is about emptying your mind."
- "Yoga's goal is to find divinity in oneself."
- "Yoga opens you up to false gods and demonic influences."
- "Yoga will be a stumbling block to your Christian witness."

Several of these common objections to Christian yoga overlap in their reasoning and philosophy, so I apologize if the following may seem a bit redundant at times. In addition, my answers to *all* the objections can be summed up in two words: Jesus Christ. Therefore this might increase the feeling of repetitiveness. But I feel this is so important because I want *you* to be confident that you are not participating in anything that is heretical, blasphemous, satanic, or otherwise dangerous to your faith. So let's take a look!

"Yoga Can't Be Separated from the Hindu Religion"

Though I've touched on this already in the book, I'll reaffirm my position here: we've already established that yoga predates Hinduism by at least one thousand years. Yoga was not created by Hindus but was indeed co-opted by Hindus as a major part of their religion. Because of this, I've heard numerous variations on the theme that yoga is inseparably bound up with Eastern religion and philosophy.

I've found that people approach yoga with a wide variety of preconceptions, such as:

- Yoga is for the purpose of becoming "one with the universe."
- Yoga leads you to find the divinity in yourself.
- Yoga is for people who are into all that "New Age stuff."

There is a nugget of truth underlying most of these notions, but none is entirely correct. First, yoga is not a religion, although various Eastern religions have adopted it as *part* of their religious practice. In particular, the Hindu religion relies heavily on ancient yoga wisdom and practice.

One way to think about the distinction between yoga and Hinduism is to consider the relationship between prayer and Christianity. Prayer is, of course, central to our lives as Christians. But most other religions utilize prayer as well. So while prayer is integral to our faith, we cannot say that prayer is only a Christian practice. Prayer is a gift of God, and humans have the discretion to decide how to use it. We do not discard prayer just because other religions use it.

Similarly, Hindus have adopted yoga as a means of spiritual and personal growth. Yet yoga, also, is a gift from God. While practitioners of the Hindu religion have used it for centuries, they cannot claim it as their own. As Christians, we may be a few millennia behind the Hindus in terms of recognizing yoga for the gift that it is, but that's no reason to stop us! We can proceed in good conscience knowing that yoga—when practiced with a totally Christ-centered intent—is a precious gift and tool that God has given us for our benefit and to enhance and facilitate our relationship with Himself. I have heard people say that yoga classes can turn Christians into Hindus or cause them to question their belief in the gospel. Again, this could be possible if you are participating in traditional yoga classes and allowing yourself to be immersed in the Eastern spiritual realm. But not Holy Yoga.

Nancy Roth puts it succinctly when she writes, "The human body does not vary according to religion."[1] This is so true! God created our bodies. He created the way we move and breathe. No single religion or cult can claim to "own" the ways we move our bodies and use them to worship our God. The postures of yoga may have been co-opted by a religion but they can't "belong" to that religion any more than prayer can belong only to a single religion. The body is of God. Prayer is of God. Scripture is of God. Other religions may have used the techniques of yoga toward their own ends, ends that conflict with a Christian worldview. They may have used yoga to worship creation or anything in it. But in Holy Yoga we worship only the Creator.

When I talk about Holy Yoga and describe how we use it to worship and connect with our Lord Jesus Christ, some people misunderstand. They think I'm trying to tell them that yoga exercises are really just "physical in nature" and that they have nothing to do with spirituality, so yoga is not dangerous to Christians. That's *not* what I'm saying. Yoga absolutely does open a person up to spiritual influences. But in Holy Yoga, the only spiritual influence we are open to is that of Jesus Christ.

Yoga *can* be separated from its Eastern history and philosophy, but we must do it intentionally, thoroughly, and carefully. We must *not* allow any heretical or sacrilegious aspects to remain (this includes the music—more on that later in the chapter). We must *completely* co-opt the amazing gift of yoga for Christianity. That's what we're doing with Holy Yoga.

"Yoga Is About Emptying Your Mind"

One of the most common concerns about yoga is that it teaches participants to "empty their minds." As Christians we tend to believe the age-old quip, "An empty mind is the devil's playground." The Bible instructs, "Be transformed by the *renewing* of your mind" (Rom. 12:2), not the *emptying* of your mind.

In Holy Yoga, though, we empty our minds of *everything but God*. We're not simply attempting to empty our minds of everything. We are creating an experience that allows for the renewing of the mind through His Word in conjunction with glorifying Him with our bodies.

As we learn to empty our minds of everything but Jesus, we are practicing giving up our selves and opening up to Him. Surrendering to God is an important theme and goal in the Christian life, and this is a vital feature of Holy Yoga. Through our practice we discover a powerful way to surrender our own thoughts and our wills to Him.

In Holy Yoga when we seek a meditative state, our purpose is to *listen to God*. Scripture tells us over one hundred times to *listen*. We are called to be still and quiet so He can direct, comfort, and grow us. We do not empty the mind, we simply make room to hear Him by disengaging from the constant inundation of life. We meditate on His Word and receive guidance for His will in our lives.

"Yoga's Goal Is to Find Divinity in Oneself"

In traditional yoga, the idea is that the divine lies within each individual, and yoga is the means to connecting with that inner divinity. As I've said, Holy Yoga is not traditional yoga. We access our wisdom, our grace, and our salvation through Christ and Christ alone.

Traditional yoga teaches one to focus on self instead of on the one true God and encourages participants to seek the answers to life's difficult questions within their own consciences instead of in the Word of God. It may leave one open to deception from God's enemy, who searches for victims that he can turn away from God.

In contrast, I believe that Holy Yoga can repel the enemy, because our hearts are so tuned to Christ that we leave no opening for the enemy.

As Christians, we know the difference between a false "divinity" within ourselves and the Almighty God. Our intent is to worship Him and Him alone.

"Yoga Opens You Up to False Gods and Demonic Influences"

A while back, I decided to take a class from a yoga teacher I used to love. He is not a Christian, but his classes had always felt "safe" to me. I even used to wish I could be as good a teacher as he was.

Unfortunately, I didn't enjoy the class as much as I'd remembered—something about it just didn't feel right. Toward the end, I noticed the music consisted of "ohm" and chanting. I was used to that—after all, I had been yoga-trained in that realm, right? During the time when I was supposed to be the most relaxed, though, lying on my mat, I found myself instead tense, guarded, and even scared. I suddenly realized how potentially compromised I was spiritually. The vibrations in the music were low and heavy and dark. In a startling moment it occurred to me that God is completely opposite of that! He is light, joy, peace—not darkness. God spoke to me and I clearly understood how Christians could very well be in danger in some traditional yoga classes. I could really feel the darkness. I grasped how Satan can use situations like that to bring people toward his darkness.

One of the reasons I was so aware of the negative influence in that yoga class is that I'd been practicing Holy Yoga for a couple of years. What a difference! While I might spend my life advocating for Holy Yoga and teaching it to Christians, *I will forever encourage everyone to participate in a yoga class that is fully Christ-centered.*

Holy Yoga is always practiced with Christian music in the background. You may choose to listen to your favorite hymns, or contemporary Christian music, or uplifting instrumental music. But we do not practice to the same music used in most secular or Eastern-influenced yoga classes.

The music used in yoga classes is designed to bring the brain into an alpha state, a deeply relaxed and calm condition. Like everything else about our bodies, the alpha state of our brain is a gift from God, in this case given to help us separate from the noisiness of the world and "be still" in our minds. I like to think of relaxation as a discipline in itself. When we allow our minds and bodies to relax, shutting out all thoughts except those of Christ, we are in effect demonstrating our complete trust in God. We are letting go of "control" and allowing ourselves to be dependent upon Him, just as we do when we go to sleep at night. Again, our focus and intent make all the difference. If we listen to music that tends to relax us while meditating on the Lord, there will be no room for demons.

What a learning experience that class was! I saw firsthand how Satan has been so effective in co-opting yoga for himself and making Christians scared of it. Satan wants to keep Christians away from a Christ-centered approach to yoga because Holy Yoga brings people closer to God! In fact, Satan has done his job so successfully that he has convinced Christians that it's *not even possible* to practice a version of yoga that's completely Christ-centered.

As Christians we are obligated to protect ourselves from Satan's influences at all times. I believe people are wise to question whether yoga can really be practiced without inviting spiritual trouble! But I also think that once people understand the difference between traditional and Holy Yoga, they will not be so fearful. I hope many people open up to this amazing way to worship and connect with Christ.

One of Satan's best weapons is fear. We have the choice to operate out of fear or love. When we reject something that is entirely for the purpose of drawing closer to Christ out of fear, we're playing right into Satan's hand. Rather than operate out of fear, we should study, discern, and seek wisdom from God.

There may be some people who should not practice Holy Yoga. If they have recently been converted from a New Age orientation and are not secure believers, then Holy Yoga is probably not the correct discipline for them. They might still be apt to take it in the wrong direction. This is similar to the discipline of fasting—which is not recommended for former anorexics, because of the danger of the spiritual fast being twisted into something no longer spiritual, and the person would end up in bondage again. This is not acting from fear but using discernment to make wise decisions.

"Yoga Will Be a Stumbling Block to Your Christian Witness"

"Be careful, however, that the exercise of your freedom does not become a stumbling block to the weak" (1 Cor. 8:9). This is an important principle to practice in our lives as Christians, no matter what we are doing. I recommend that if you are going to take up yoga, be sure to practice Holy Yoga or another overtly Christ-centered yoga. Do your homework. Sit in on a class before participating if necessary. But make sure you're not harming your own witness by taking part in yoga that can be compromising.

Still, others may question you, and a weaker brother may misunderstand and think it's acceptable to participate in activities that mingle Eastern and New Age philosophies with Christianity. You are going to want to always be clear that you practice yoga as a means of connecting with Christ.

Interestingly, other disciplines can affect a person's witness as well. Fasting is a notable example. Nonbelievers look upon people who undertake long-term spiritual fasts as "crazy," and often even believers ridicule them. The way to maintain your positive Christian witness and not become a stumbling block is all in your attitude. Are you filled with love and reflecting Christ in your daily behavior? Are you constantly glorifying the name of our Almighty God? Are you humble about your endeavor? If so, then the chance of your being a stumbling block is slim.

"But thanks be to God, who always leads us in triumphal procession in Christ and through us spreads everywhere the fragrance of the knowledge of him. For we are to God the aroma of Christ among those who are being saved and those who are perishing" (2 Cor. 2:14–15). Let's continually strive to be the beautiful aroma of Christ.

There may be other objections to Holy Yoga that I've not addressed here. But you don't need me to talk about each and every one of them. If you come up against a concern, an argument, or a criticism that merits your attention, take it seriously. Consider it. Search the Bible for help. Pray about it. And finally, remember that in Holy Yoga, the answer to practically every question is two words: Jesus Christ.

CHAPTER 5

The Holy Yoga Lifestyle

Look to the LORD and his strength; seek his face always.
1 Chronicles 16:11

My friends Dawn and Gavin have been practicing Holy Yoga with me for the last couple of years. They are the parents of four children and own two businesses. Dawn says,

> Our lives are very hectic, and we have difficulty finding time for the things that are so important to us: Christ, our health, and each other. Holy Yoga enables us to really connect . . . to Christ, our bodies, our minds, and each other . . . in such a complete and fulfilling way. Holy Yoga has become part of our Tuesday date night ritual and we can't think of a better way to start the night! I feel as if something is missing if we can't make it for some reason.

I love how Dawn and Gavin have made Holy Yoga an integral part of their lives, not just an appointment on their to-do list. Holy Yoga is not only a break for exercise, praise, and worship—it's a lifestyle.

When you talk with yoga teachers or experienced practitioners, it's common to hear them talk about their "yoga lifestyle." As

Larry Payne says, "The practice of yoga has a way of seeping into other parts of your life. For most people, it helps cultivate greater awareness; slows down the pace, increases enjoyment of simple, everyday activities; and generally improves their outlook."[1]

Does this sound familiar at all? To me, it sounds like what my walk with God does. When I am taking time to be with Him every day in prayer and in the Word, it doesn't just affect me during those "quiet times" or in church on Sunday. It seeps into every moment of every day. While the yoga lifestyle involves adhering to certain principles throughout each day, the Holy Yoga lifestyle is really a Christ-centered lifestyle. It's about remaining connected to our Lord and Savior in our daily lives, no matter what we are doing.

Practicing the Presence

Brother Lawrence's classic book, *Practicing the Presence of God,* tells how this seventeenth-century monk cultivated a completely God-focused way of life. In a modern-day translation of his work, he expresses, "I don't know of a better, sweeter life than an unbroken conversation with God, a life of unlimited free minutes with Him."[2] That, in essence, is what it means to bring the essence of Holy Yoga into daily life.

Brother Lawrence goes on to say,

> When we stay focused on God in His presence, it gets harder to disappoint Him or do things He doesn't want . . . at least on purpose. We discover a holy freedom to go to the Lord for everything we need—the breath to breathe for Him, the life to live for Him, the grace to keep going. After a while, with practice, being in God's presence this way becomes a totally natural habit.[3]

Of course, we are always in God's presence. As David expressed it, "Where can I go from your Spirit? Where can I flee from your presence? If I go up to the heavens, you are there; if I make my bed in the depths, you are there" (Ps. 139:7–8). God is always with us. The question is whether we allow ourselves—or discipline ourselves—to be constantly *aware* of His presence.

Exactly how do we practice the presence of God throughout our days? Of course, entire books have been written and countless sermons preached on the topic. So I am merely going to highlight five principles we can use to briefly illustrate how we can allow the practice of Holy Yoga to seep into daily life by striving to stay present with the Lord.

The Holy Yoga Lifestyle

1. Pray Without Ceasing

Paul exhorted us in his to-the-point style to "pray continually" (1 Thess. 5:17). This is the best way to keep ourselves focused on God, not ourselves. When we practice Holy Yoga, one of our central objectives is to learn to get away from the "it's all about me" way of life. We live in a culture that loves excess. We need *more*—more time, more money, more stuff. Not only do we "need" more but we have been taught that we are entitled to have more—and have it "our way."

As I write this, I am smack-dab in the center of a Bible study on Daniel. In the study we've explored how our modern-day Western culture parallels the ancient Babylonian culture's way of thinking that "I am, and there is none besides me" (Isa. 47:10). I began to wonder, *Are we really so disconnected from continual dialogue with God? Have we gotten away from His will and been overtaken by our own? Have I?*

My eyes were opened to just how engrained this was when I found myself at Starbucks one morning. There were two people in front of me, so already I was on edge. I mean, really now—how hard would it be to hire another barista? I clearly hadn't had my fix yet. When I got to the counter, I ordered my favorite: a venti, nonfat, two-pump, sugar-free vanilla, half-caf latte with extra foam. Oh, and I almost forgot—extra hot with "driving room."

As I shelled out my $4.91, it hit me like a ton of coffee beans. What? What did I just say? This is a cup of coffee we are talking about, right? Am I really that self-absorbed? Now I usually order my coffee black while praising God as I wait in line for that one barista behind the counter.

We need to spend time learning to direct our awareness toward God and away from self. In Holy Yoga, even as we are using our bodies to worship, paying attention to the positioning of our limbs, heeding any sensations of pain, we are directing our thoughts and actions toward Him.

Mother Teresa said, "We must be aware of oneness with Christ, as he was aware of oneness with his Father."[4] That constant awareness in itself functions as prayer, as we develop the habit of unbroken conversation with our continual Companion.

One of the ways I have learned to understand this concept is by having children. As the mom of three little ones, I have no shortage of continual companions! My responsibility for them requires that I maintain constant awareness of them, while my love makes it impossible for me *not* to. I might be preparing a meal or working on the computer with my children nearby, and I have one eye on them. Or I might be somewhere else—out with my husband, or teaching a Holy Yoga class—but still, my heart is inclined toward my children. They come to mind frequently, I'm concerned for their welfare, and I look forward to being with them again.

I think that's what it means to practice God's presence! No matter what we're doing, we are to be aware of Him as companion, sharing with him our thoughts and feelings, avoiding becoming obsessed with self and instead inclining our hearts toward Him.

In addition, we can occasionally stop whatever we're doing and take a moment to be still, and know that He is God.

2. Confess, Repent, and Forgive

When we carry around unconfessed sin, it weighs down our spirits. David expressed it perfectly in Psalm 32:

> For day and night
>   your hand was heavy upon me;
>   my strength was sapped
>   as in the heat of summer.
>   . . . Then I acknowledged my sin to you
>   and did not cover up my iniquity.
>   I said, "I will confess
>   my transgressions to the LORD"—
> and you forgave the guilt of my sin. (vv. 4–5)

There is no greater relief, and I think there is no gift more incomprehensible and amazing, than having our sins forgiven. And there is nothing that separates us from God more readily than carrying around unconfessed sin. Daily confession—hourly, if necessary!—is a way to constantly remain close to our Savior, as we rest in His forgiveness.

Along with confession comes *repentance*. Mark Buchanan, in his lovely book *The Rest of God*, gives an insightful definition of the word: "Repentance is a ruthless dismantling of old ways of seeing and thinking, and then a diligent and vigilant building of new ones."[5] All of us have areas of sin in our lives, whether it be our thoughts, our words, or our actions. If we make the effort to uncompromisingly pry loose those old habits and intentionally replace them with new ones, we can be sure that God will be with us in that process.

The Lord spoke through Isaiah when He said, "In repentance and rest is your salvation" (30:15). I love how those two words go together—*repentance* and *rest*. When we repent, we can rest in the Lord. We can't rest peacefully in God's presence if we haven't repented, and so the continual process of repentance is key to staying close to Him in our daily lives.

When we confess and repent, God forgives us. "As far as the east is from the west, so far has he removed our transgressions from us" (Ps. 103:12). What an amazing thing! I was always able to intellectually comprehend God's forgiveness. But God's forgiveness is experiential. It is God's main desire to have an intimate relationship with us and so I believe we are given ample opportunities to experience Him.

When I began having an intimate relationship with Christ, we had some work to do! I needed some serious loosening of my bonds. I needed freedom. I needed a Savior. God not only blessed me with His forgiveness but through that relationship showed me how I could forgive myself.

To be authentically free in Christ means just that: to be free from the bonds we place on ourselves through guilt, shame, resentment, and unforgiveness. God gave His Son to be our sacrificial lamb, to cover all of our sins so that we may be free. Isaiah 43:25 says "I am He who blots out your transgressions, for my own sake, and remembers your sins no more." Our transgressions, when rectified by repentance, are for *His* glory. It is about time we let ourselves experience authentic, godly forgiveness.

God's forgiveness goes one step farther and obligates us to forgive others as well: "If you do not forgive men their sins, your Father will not forgive your sins" (Matt. 6:15). Jesus didn't give us these words to make life harder. Carrying around anger and blame is actually one of the things that make life more difficult, weighing us down the same way unconfessed sin does. Practicing forgiveness, for all the inconsequential things as well as the significant ones, is an important way to practice a Christ-centered lifestyle.

3. Cultivate Contentment

Brother Lawrence wrote, "My priority is to be in God's presence—and stay there. . . . This is where I find joy and how I stay content."[6] It's interesting to me that practicing God's presence is a way to cultivate contentment—and cultivating contentment is a way to practice God's presence.

I believe contentment comes from a spirit of gratitude. If we are focusing on the things we are thankful for rather than on the things we don't have, it sure goes a long way toward lifting our spirits! Kathleen Norris wrote, "Prayer is not asking for what you want but asking to be changed in ways you can't imagine. To be made more grateful, more able to see the good in what you have been given instead of always grieving for what might have been."[7] She acknowledged that on our own, we won't always be as thankful as we should be and we may have a difficult time feeling content. But we can pray to be made more grateful, and we can pray to be given new eyes to see the blessing of what's right in front of us.

When the apostle Paul said that he'd learned to be content in all circumstances (Phil. 4:11), he didn't mean he was gritting his teeth, clenching his fists, and pretending to be happy. He meant that he truly felt peaceful and provided for. He also gave us the secret to this deep and authentic satisfaction: "I can do everything through him who gives me strength" (Phil. 4:13). Knowing that we can trust in God for anything we ever need is the key to cultivating contentment.

I always encourage my classes not to "rush the sweet stuff." I ask them to sit in stillness and call on God to sustain them in it. Most tend to rush through their prayer and meditation time. What if it is the only time that day they really experience the presence and contentment of God?

What is the rush? Your to-do list is still waiting for you and the house is still a wreck whether you rest a moment or not. We are reminded in Philippians 4:6–7 that we should "not be anxious about anything but in everything, by prayer and petition, with thanksgiving, present your requests to God. And the peace of God, which transcends all understanding, will guard your hearts and minds in Christ Jesus."

Now that, my friends, is an awesome recipe for contentment. Sit and rest in that for a moment. Don't rush the sweet stuff.

4. Practice Obedience

Jesus taught, "If anyone loves me, he will obey my teaching" (John 14:23). I believe this is an important part of bringing the Holy Yoga mind-set into our daily lives. If we strive to adhere to the principles He taught, we will find ourselves naturally gravitating toward a closer relationship with Him.

As Christians, sometimes it seems we are shockingly unmindful of the magnitude of obedience. Jerry Bridges points out that we can't simply pray for holiness, we have to pursue it through our submission to God's Word.[8] Practicing obedience means intentionally seeking throughout each day to exhibit behaviors—outwardly *and* inwardly—that reflect Jesus Christ.

Before I became a Christian, I thought God was all about the rules. I thought of myself as someone who didn't really "do" rules. I wasn't up for donning a prairie dress complete with matching bonnet and living in a church pew. That was what God wanted, right? Perfect people living perfect lives. That was my idea of a Christian and I had things to do, people to see!

Once I asked Jesus into my heart, I began to realize that these rules were not so hard to follow at all. Of course, I learned they were not rules at all. The more I became friends with my Savior, the more I longed to please Him. I came to understand that these "rules" were for my own well-being so that He could create in me a clean heart and bestow upon me His will for my life. I learned obedience is an offering of a grateful heart. It is the action of thanking God for His grace and the beauty that He has breathed into my very being. Second John 1:6 says, "And this is love: that we walk in obedience to his commands." I do now spend a lot of time in a pew—thankfully bonnet-free.

A. W. Tozer wrote, "Prayer will become effective when we stop using it as a substitute for obedience."[9] Ouch! He saw that we often pray that we will obey—we pray for patience, for compassion, or that we would be free from covetousness—yet we do not take the actions necessary to actually abide by Christ's teachings in those areas.

Are you praying for anything that you might bring to realization through obedience? What are some of the areas in which God might be asking you to obey?

5. Do Everything with Love

When Jesus was asked which of the commandments were most important, He responded, "Love the Lord your God with all your heart and with all your soul and with all your mind and with all your strength" (Mark 12:30). We've already spent considerable time on that verse, but Jesus also gave a second command: "Love your neighbor as yourself" (Mark 12:31). This sums up a good deal of the teachings in the New Testament. Jesus was all about love, and the story of God is a story of God's unfailing love for His people.

God's love is the motivation and the example for our love of others. Later, Paul wrote, "If I have a faith that can move mountains, but have not love, I am nothing. If I give all I possess to the poor and surrender my body to the flames, but have not love, I gain nothing" (1 Cor. 13:2–3). In other words, love is the answer to everything. Love ties us to God, and to one another. Love makes our obedience possible; it allows us to put God and others before ourselves.

Sometimes the idea of doing everything with love seems a bit vague, doesn't it? Whenever we need a little guidance in that area, 1 Corinthians 13 can be our guide. Ask yourself: *Have I* been patient with my children? Was I kind to the person who was rude to me? Do I envy those with nicer houses or cars—or those who seem more "spiritual" than I am? Did I boast about my success at work? Are there areas of pride in my life that need to be addressed?

The apostle Paul's descriptions of love continue, but you get the picture. Doing everything with love is not vague at all. The instructions are right there. As you connect to your Source of love, you treat others with the love of God that shines through you. In turn you will be aware of His presence and experience the rich blessings of a life lived fully in Christ.

The Fruit of Your Endeavors

Practicing God's presence through all of these means is a way of living that helps us to reflect Christ to others as we grow in our relationship with Him. Doing Holy Yoga can help us in this pursuit because of the way it can help us feel centered, peaceful, and healthy. My students often comment on how they carry this feeling out of class and everywhere they go. They worry less about trivial problems, they are able to focus more fully on others with whom they communicate, and they find themselves generally more receptive to God.

If you're ever wondering how well you're doing at living a Christ-centered lifestyle, take a look at Galatians 5:22–23 and study what the fruit of the Spirit looks like: love, joy, peace, patience, kindness, goodness, faithfulness, gentleness, and self-control. Ask yourself how well these virtues are being exhibited in your life.

In nature, fruit is the sweet result of lots of hard work—sowing, tending, pruning, harvesting. But the fruit of a plant is also its reproductive body; in other words, the fruit is the means by which the plant reproduces itself. So doesn't that imply that when we exhibit the fruit of the Spirit, that we are the means by which the Holy Spirit is reproduced, multiplied, and spread around to others?

That's the greatest thing about Holy Yoga. It puts us in a place where the Lord can work in and through us, so that we better reveal the fruit of the Spirit—and hopefully bring more people to His feet. What could be better than that?

PART TWO

Yoga—God's Provision for Good Health

CHAPTER 6

How Yoga Benefits Your Mind and Body

Heal me, O Lord, and I will be healed; save me and I will be saved,
for you are the one I praise.
Jeremiah 17:14

I don't know about you, but as my body ages, I find myself experiencing little "surprises" more and more often: feeling tired when I thought I had gotten enough sleep; a sore muscle where I never had one before; occasional bouts of depression or insecurity; and increased stress as life continues to spiral around me. Especially after having three children, my body just isn't what it used to be—not in yoga, not on the treadmill, and certainly not in a bikini! I find myself looking for ways to ensure my health and prevent as many "surprises" as possible.

In addition to my own experience, I know many people suffer from more than just normal aging. Chronic diseases, bad knees, heart problems, digestive disorders—the list of ailments never seems to end and we're all at risk for developing something major in our lifetimes. It's obvious we can't stop all of these assaults on our health. But there are ways we can maintain our general health as well as manage many of our illnesses and disorders. Yoga is one of the best-known and well-substantiated ways to do that.

In the last few chapters we've talked about the many ways yoga can be used as a discipline in our Christian walk. Yoga teaches us to focus more deeply in prayer and use our entire beings to praise and worship God. It's clearly a blessing that deeply enhances our spiritual lives. But I know you've picked up this book for more than just the spiritual aspects of yoga—you also want to know how it can benefit your body, mind, emotions, and overall health! While entire books have been written on this topic, I'm going to spend this one chapter outlining the basics of how yoga can be a tremendous advantage in keeping your body and mind healthy.

Yoga practitioners have always been aware of yoga's role in maintaining good overall health. Of course, we live in an era where people accept few things unless they have been scientifically proven. So over the last few decades, scientists and medical doctors have subjected yoga to rigorous study. Not surprisingly, what people's bodies have been telling them for centuries, science is now finally confirming. Physicians and scientists are discovering new health benefits of yoga every day. Studies show that regular practice of movement, breath work, and meditation help relieve the symptoms of illnesses such as arthritis, arteriosclerosis, chronic fatigue, diabetes, high blood pressure, digestive disorders, asthma, and even varicose veins.

These and many other conditions are serious problems for Americans. But perhaps the most widespread complaint, shared by men and women of all ages, is stress. Let's start by taking a look at modern-day stress and how yoga can help.

Stressed-Out Lives

I know very few people who would say their lives aren't characterized by a high level of stress on a frequent basis. A certain degree of stress is natural, necessary, and not harmful, yet most of us would agree that we experience too much stress! Think about it for a moment. Do you feel stressed sometimes? Often? Always?

What does being stressed feel like? For some, it's a chronic state of anxiety or worry. For others, it feels like a consistent lack of peace in their mental and emotional state—the feeling everything is always jumbled, there is too much to do and not enough resources with which to do it. Thanks to our desire for more, we always seem to be lacking in time or energy to actually enjoy all the "more" we have.

How does stress manifest itself physically in your life? You might feel it as tense muscles, poor sleeping habits, unhealthful eating patterns, or general irritability. You might be surprised to know that stress affects our bodies in hundreds of ways that we aren't even aware of. It affects the inner workings of the body all the way down to the cellular level. Every bodily system—respiratory, digestive, muscular, cardiovascular, and lymphatic—is affected by whether our bodies and minds are stressed or relatively relaxed.

Stress is the body's common response to threat—any type of threat, *whether real or imagined.* Of course, God gave us our stress reaction for very good reasons! It heightens our awareness and enables us to react to danger quickly and effectively. On the physical level, a stress response includes adrenaline flowing into the bloodstream, increased heart rate, rapid breathing, and tightened muscles. If you have ever been threatened by an enormous and immediate physical danger, you might remember your body reacting this way. What a blessing! Our bodies are perfectly equipped to respond to jeopardy with all our senses heightened and our muscles ready to take action.

It becomes a problem, however, when we exist in a continual state of stress. Our bodies were designed to cope with these short periods of stress and then release the stress through physical action. But if we have chronic long-term stress without the appropriate physical release, the toll it takes on our bodily systems is tremendous.

Muscles remain in that tightened state, the heart beats too rapidly for long periods of time, breathing is often shallow and erratic. Another interesting response during stress is that nonessential bodily systems are slowed down in order for the body to send all its resources to the parts that need it. The digestive system is one that gets slowed down, and so you can see why chronic stress commonly leads to digestive problems. Stress trains our bodies to have poor digestion!

Along with the physical changes brought by stress itself are the more subtle behavioral changes that accompany stress: eating less healthfully, exercising less, and engaging in more high-risk behaviors such as drinking and smoking.[1] By now it should be obvious that we need a way to reduce stress in our lives!

How Yoga Helps Relieve Stress

"The most direct way to de-stress is to take two or three slow, deep breaths whenever you notice that you are anxious or under strain. . . . By paying attention to your breathing, you can switch off the stressed part of your nervous system and return to a state of calm."[2] So says Dr. Frederic Luskin, coauthor of *Stress Free for Good*. Numerous studies validate this very simple concept. Since a major component of yoga is slow, mindful breathing, we can see right away how the regular practice of yoga can begin to bring a sense of calm to our lives. Fitness expert Rich Weil has reviewed major scientific studies and verified that yoga practitioners show both lower perceived stress and a reduced blood pressure and heart rate.[3]

In addition to the calming effects of mindful breathing, the unhurried stretching of the muscles and the slow, deliberate movement of the joints reduces tension held throughout the body.

Holy Yoga also teaches a state of mind that can in itself reduce stress. It helps us learn to be in the moment and to focus on God's truth in that moment. Carried throughout your day, that habit can make a huge difference in the level of stress you perceive in any given situation. If we've learned to focus on God—His truth, His strength, His grace—and lay our burdens at His feet, we will also decrease our daily stress load.

Many Christians believe that since we have the advantage of relationship with Christ, we shouldn't fall prey to stress the way nonbelievers do. Unfortunately, Christians experience stress at the same rate as the general population. According to *Relevant Magazine,* "The Christian community as a whole needs to acknowledge that stress is a truly human condition. What Christianity offers is a means of lessening the negative effects of stress in a person's life through a relationship with a God who promises to give us rest."[4]

I think it's especially important that we, as Christians, pay attention to our stress levels and make sure they don't get out of control. Stress can diminish our relationship with Christ in so many ways. It makes us feel as if we don't have time for Him. It robs us of the peace He wants to give us. It leads us into all manner of negative behaviors and even into sin. Practicing Holy Yoga is one good way to protect ourselves from becoming overwhelmed by the day-to-day stresses in this life.

But stress isn't the only health hazard that yoga can help us alleviate. Let's take a look at some of the others.

Physiological Benefits of Yoga

Most people are aware of the innumerable health benefits yoga practitioners claim. But the advantages of yoga have gone far beyond the anecdotal—they've been documented for years now. Here are some of the most important ways yoga helps maintain health and manage common ailments.

Normal Aging

"Yoga counters the effects of the aging process by moving each joint in the body through its full range of motion—stretching, strengthening, and balancing each part," notes Suza Francina, yoga teacher and author of *The New Yoga for People Over Fifty*. She explains that age-related musculoskeletal diseases like osteoporosis, osteoarthritis, and carpal tunnel syndrome respond well to yoga's weight-bearing postures. Especially helpful are the inverted postures in which the arms, wrists, and hands are strengthened. While many of the usual forms of weight-bearing exercise can increase stiffness, yoga includes both stretching and strengthening to relieve stiff joints and muscles.[5]

Normal aging often includes digestive troubles, which are aided by yoga. The conscious and careful twisting of the torso combined with stretching of the surrounding muscles helps to keep those digestive organs in their best shape.

Back Pain

Back pain is a common reason people seek medical attention. Both acute and long-term stress can lead to muscle tension and exacerbate back problems. Yoga has consistently been used to cure and prevent back pain by enhancing strength and flexibility.[6]

Arthritis

Yoga's slow-motion movements and gentle pressures reach deep into troubled joints. In addition, the easy stretches in conjunction with deep-breathing exercises relieve the tension that binds up the muscles and further tightens the joints. Yoga is exercise and relaxation rolled into one—an effective antiarthritis formula.

Asthma

Numerous studies have proven yoga's effectiveness in managing asthma, even to the point of preventing asthma attacks without using medication. One study showed that a fifteen-week yoga program significantly improved overall lung functioning. Even a brief yoga program can have a significant effect on asthma, reducing attacks and lessening reliance on medication and inhalers.[7] (But never decrease or stop use of prescribed medication without checking with your doctor first.)

Physicians have found some good reasons for these positive effects on the respiratory system. Studies have shown that yoga increases people's flow rate (the rate of air going in and out of the lungs) as well as their vital capacity (the amount of air you can inhale at one time). Improvements in these important facets of the respiratory system naturally stem many of the symptoms of asthma and other respiratory ailments.

High Blood Pressure

The relaxation and exercise components of yoga can play a major role in the treatment and prevention of high blood pressure (hypertension). Research published in the April 2000 issue of *Indian Journal of Physiology and Pharmacology* showed that yoga may be as effective as drug therapy in controlling hypertension.[8] Study after study has shown reduced blood pressure and improved recovery from other heart ailments like coronary artery disease simply from adding a brief yoga routine to the daily schedule.

If you've dealt with cardiovascular problems, you probably know that the medications used to treat them are rife with unpleasant side effects. A regular practice of yoga can reduce or even eliminate the need for these medications. (Again, though, don't decrease or stop use of prescribed medication without checking with your doctor first.)

Pain Management

Yoga is believed to reduce pain by helping the brain's pain center regulate the secretion of natural painkillers in the body. Breathing exercises used in yoga can also reduce pain by producing relaxation and reducing tension. Part of the effectiveness of yoga in alleviating pain is the way it trains you to listen to your body. This valuable skill can have a protective effect and allow for early preventive action.

Weight Reduction

Regular yoga practice can help in weight management. Some of the postures stimulate sluggish glands to increase their hormonal secretions. The thyroid gland, especially, has a big effect on our weight because it affects body metabolism. Several postures, such as the shoulder stand and the fish posture, are specifically for the thyroid gland. Fat metabolism is also increased, so fat is converted to muscle and energy. This means that, as well as losing fat, you will have better muscle tone and a higher vitality level. In addition, yoga practices that reduce anxiety tend to reduce anxious eating, which naturally helps with weight loss or maintenance.

Preparation for Other Physical Activities

Perhaps you're generally healthy and not too worried about ailments or aging yet. If you're active and involved in sports or other physical activities, you can keep your muscles and joints flexible through yoga. For runners and joggers, yoga counters the effects of gravity from the repeated high-impact on the body. If you take part in asymmetric sports (twisting the spine in only one direction) such as tennis or golf, yoga helps to restore symmetry to the body.

"Yoga also supplies flexibility that can help in safely practicing power sports and weight training," according to Dr. Julio Kuperman, associate professor at the University of Pennsylvania School of Medicine.[9] If you enjoy skiing or snowboarding, horseback riding, backpacking, or other sports that challenge your body physically, you significantly reduce your risk of injury by staying flexible and strong through yoga.

Mental/Emotional Benefits

It's hard to overestimate the effect yoga can have on a person's mental and emotional state. The relaxing and stress-reducing effect alone is enough to bring about a noticeable difference in quality of life.

Mental health and physical energy are difficult to quantify, but virtually everyone who participates in yoga over a period of time reports a positive effect on outlook and energy level. Yoga stretching and breathing exercises have been seen to result in an invigorating effect on both mental and physical energy and improved mood. Regular yoga practice creates mental clarity and calmness, increases body awareness, relieves chronic stress patterns, relaxes the mind, centers attention, and sharpens concentration.

While you are practicing yoga, you will be learning to improve your focus and concentration. While focusing on Christ, you'll also be concentrating on your body position. There is no room for distraction, so the mind is progressively trained to remain calm and pay attention. This can't help but spill over into daily life, translating into a generally more relaxed and positive outlook on life.

Holy Yoga has a unique advantage over other types of yoga practice in that it allows us to create time and space for our Creator. We actively seek Him, spend time with Him, and listen for His voice. No matter what our emotional or mental state, this time with Him is crucial for our spiritual development and will lead us to rest in His arms no matter what we are going through.

Putting It All Together

This chapter has been about how yoga affects our minds and bodies, but let's not forget how all of this ties in with our relationship with our Savior. When I began to practice Holy Yoga, it really helped me to understand and experience the sacredness of this body that He created. For the first time ever, I had a deep sense of the completely amazing fact that *God created me.* He created each of us *in His image*—every joint and muscle, every bone and limb, built for His glory.

Practicing Holy Yoga has given me a deep desire to worship and praise God evermore, with all that I am, because I have a clearer appreciation of the incredible gift of my body, mind, and spirit. It causes me to sing in the words of David, "For you created my inmost being; you knit me together in my mother's womb. I praise you because I am fearfully and wonderfully made" (Ps. 139:13–14). Let's appreciate how amazing it is that we are His hands and His feet.

One of my students, Tom, said,

> Not only does the earth spin pretty fast, but I'm wound pretty tight. Holy Yoga . . . has a special way of slowing down time and helping my overactive mind decompress, unwind, and reconnect to its true Source. The impact on my underactive body has been profound in terms of strength and flexibility. My connection to God is getting better with time, but rarely is it stronger than during Holy Yoga.

I think Tom has really put it all together. Yoga's effects on mind, body, and spirit can be truly life-changing. Those effects can be present not only during yoga practice, but throughout the remainder of our daily lives. In the next chapter we'll take a look at how that happens.

CHAPTER 7

When, Where, and How?

Prepare the way for the Lord, make straight paths for him.
Mark 1:3

*A*fter all this time we've spent talking about Holy Yoga and the countless ways it can enhance your life, I hope you're sitting on the edge of your seat, thinking, *Enough already! Let's do some yoga!* We're almost ready. In this chapter we'll address the basics of when, where, and how to get your practice going.

I'll begin by telling you about the three basic components of yoga: breathing, meditation, and postures. After that I'll give you tips on finding the right time and space for your practice and what you'll need. Then we'll talk about the mind-set necessary to begin your Holy Yoga journey, and we'll finish up with some important physical guidelines you'll need to keep in mind throughout your practice.

The Three Components of Holy Yoga

1. The Breath

Recently my friend Denise (not her real name) had an experience that got her blood boiling. She'd gone away overnight with her husband to celebrate their anniversary and come home to find that their neighbor had neglected to care for their puppy as agreed. I'll leave out the details, but the house was a mess and didn't smell very pleasant! Normally even-tempered, Denise erupted into a rage. She remembered the time and effort she'd spent taking care of the neighbor's dogs. She couldn't believe her neighbor had been so thoughtless! Her body was shaking, her heart was racing, and her breathing was rapid. Denise knew she was out of control. She wanted to march next door and give that neighbor a piece of her mind.

Instead, Denise decided to take a five-minute breathing break (at the prodding of her husband). She sat down and practiced five minutes of a simple yoga technique called Focused Breathing while repeating a brief prayer for God's peace. Within moments, she stopped shaking and she felt her pulse returning to normal. Her anger abated, she entered a state of calm, and she was able to resolve the situation peacefully with no blame or recrimination, and no hard feelings between neighbors.

Such is the power of the breath! Focused Breathing is the most crucial aspect of Holy Yoga. It can be used anytime and anywhere, and it is always used while practicing yoga. There are several techniques of yoga breathing and they all increase our ability to focus on a desired point of attention, which during Holy Yoga is twofold: God and the movement of our bodies. Other types of yoga breathing can induce a state of calm, energize the mind and body, provide a balancing effect to your system, relax the body, bring pain relief, or even quiet pangs of hunger. In chapter 8 I will introduce you to a few different types of yoga breathing techniques.

2. Meditation

When I first started doing yoga and I mentioned meditation as part of the practice, people invariably closed their eyes, put their thumbs and middle fingers together in a circle, and eventually began chanting, "Oohhhhmmm." It always made me laugh because that's the view most of us have of meditation! Many Christians are not aware that meditation has long been used as a classical Christian discipline and a means of deepening one's relationship with God.

I am going to teach you some methods of meditation in chapter 9 so that you will have it available to you as one more way to bring your mind and body in harmony with each other and with God. Meditation can bring you into a deep focus on our Lord at the same time that it relaxes the mind and clears away the stresses of the day. But it's not easy! In fact, I think meditation is one of the more challenging of the Christian disciplines and definitely a difficult aspect of Holy Yoga. Its rewards can be great, though, so I encourage you to try it.

3. Yoga Postures

At last we come to the part of yoga that everyone knows something about: the bending, twisting, touching-your-toes, and standing-on-your-head part of yoga. (Except we're not going to stand on our heads quite yet!) I routinely hear "Oh no, not yoga. I can't even touch my toes!" My response is always the same: "Well then, there is no candidate better than you to come to class!"

The postures constitute the third major element of any yoga program. The second half of this book is entirely devoted to teaching you a wide variety of yoga poses: standing, sitting, balancing, inverted, twisting, bending, and relaxing postures. Each type of yoga position and movement has a unique purpose and effect, and in a yoga practice they are combined in specific ways to keep your body balanced, aligned, and flexible. Later in the book as we introduce each type of yoga posture, I'll share with you a bit about each one's objective. Now let's turn to some things you need to know before starting your yoga practice.

The Basics of Time, Place, and Supplies

By far the biggest obstacle for most of us in sticking to a regular exercise schedule or a consistent devotional commitment is that we are too busy and we feel as if we have no time. As a busy wife and mother with a career and a ministry, I'm no stranger to this problem! I've found that the best way to fit these important elements into daily life is to first, try to develop a habit, and second, go easy on myself. Guilt won't do anything to help us, and neither will anger at ourselves or sinking into a feeling of failure. Ease into this new lifestyle gently, giving yourself grace.

Time

Traditionally throughout the ages, yoga has most often been practiced first thing in the morning upon waking. Interestingly, that's the time most Christians choose to pray, read the Bible, and spend time with the Lord. Because of the way Holy Yoga combines bodily exercise with devotional time, I believe first thing in the morning is a fantastic time to practice. You'll need to find the best time that works for your schedule. The most important factors in choosing a time to practice are:

The consistency of the time of day. If possible, choose a time during which you're able to do Holy Yoga most days. Consistency helps to build habit.

Not too soon after a big meal. Allow two to three hours. But a light snack about an hour before your practice can be beneficial.

Start small. If you don't have much time available, carve out twenty minutes, two or three times a week, and plan to stick with this schedule for a few weeks. Gradually, as you become accustomed to doing yoga, you will be able to increase the length of each session and perhaps add a couple more sessions per week.

Choose a time in which you are least likely to be interrupted. It's important to "protect" this time as best you can. Ask your spouse or housemates for their understanding, and try not to be the one responsible for children at that time. For me, this is nearly impossible! That's why I find myself rising extremely early in the morning, while the rest of the family is sleeping, to have my special time alone with God. (Of course, even this doesn't always work. My children seem to have frequent five a.m. "nightmares" or longings for cuddle sessions that are simply impossible to turn down!)

Place

It's important to choose a place to practice in which you feel comfortable. The temperature should not be too warm or cool, and it should be relatively private, with a closed door to prevent interruptions. You also need to make sure you have enough space to maneuver without injuring yourself on furniture or other items lying around. If you're going to practice Holy Yoga at home, take a few minutes to consider different spaces. Sit on the floor, look around, and see how you feel. Make an intentional choice and mentally label it your own personal Holy Yoga spot.

I have a friend who practices in her basement, which is really the children's playroom and is constantly strewn with toys. But she has added touches to make it her own when the kids aren't around—a stereo to play Christian music, and a basket to hold her yoga props and supplies. She also has made it a habit to straighten up the playroom each night before she goes to sleep so that it officially becomes her "yoga room" for the morning. (Who would have thought that Holy Yoga would also be a motivation for housekeeping?) Having a designated yoga spot helps keep my friend inspired to get up early each morning and practice!

I love to practice outdoors whenever possible. It is so amazing to be touching the earth in the natural light with clean, fresh air oxygenating all the systems of my body. Next time you have the chance, roll your mat out on your lawn or even on your porch and praise Him for all the majesty in His making!

Supplies

There are a few things you'll need to be comfortable practicing yoga. Keep in mind that each of these items is subject to your personal needs and preferences. At the start, take an experimental approach, and be open to finding what works for you. Here is what I recommend to get started:

Proper clothing. There's no specific attire needed for practicing yoga. You'll need to figure out your own preferences by trial and error. Generally, your clothes need to be comfortable and allow uninhibited movement. Loose-fitting is good, but not too loose! (Another friend enjoyed practicing first thing in the morning in her pajamas. She soon stopped doing that—her baggy pj's became a real problem during inverted poses!) Be aware of the temperature of your environment, and dress accordingly. Remember that your body will warm up as you get into your routine, so if you need to start with a light extra layer that you can shed, that works fine.

Yoga mat or rug. This is the only official "yoga" product I suggest you consider purchasing. Yoga mats are often referred to as "sticky mats" because they are padded yet have a tacky surface that keeps you from sliding around in the middle of a pose. At the beginning, you can try practicing on carpet, or on a towel. If you decide to go in search of a yoga mat, they are readily available at most sporting goods stores and even general merchandise stores. They're also plentiful online. How much you spend will depend on your preference and budget, but I've seen them range in price from ten to seventy-five dollars.

Towel and blanket. Towels and blankets come in handy during yoga practice for a variety of uses. You may need a towel to wipe perspiration or to roll up and use as a bolster to aide in certain postures. A throw blanket comes in handy for the relaxation portion of your practice—it's much easier to relax if you're not feeling a chill. You can also use a rolled-up blanket as a pillow or a prop.

Bottle or glass of water. Good to have handy for small sips during your practice and to rehydrate after your session.

CD or DVD player. Make sure your yoga space can accommodate whatever technology you're going to use during your practice. (Note: Some people try to do yoga with headphones and an MP3 player. I don't recommend this as it hampers your movement and is too distracting.)

Props

In addition to the supplies I've listed, you might want some items that are traditionally called *yoga props*. Some of the postures in this book call for the following props:

Block. A block is usually made of wood or of sturdy foam and measures about nine inches high, six inches wide, and four inches deep. These are used to support different parts of your body during certain poses. If you don't want to start off buying a block, you can use a small stack of sturdy books or some other type of durable box of the right size. One or two blocks will suffice for any practice.

Bolster. These are large, firm, rectangular, or oval pillows used to support your knees, neck, or upper back. Bolsters can be expensive, so it's fine to begin your practice by making your own bolsters out of thickly rolled blankets. Sometimes even a sofa pillow or bed pillow will work, but not if it's too soft. Again, experiment to see what works for you.

Strap. A yoga strap—or belt—extends your reach and lets you increase or maintain leg and arm stretches. If you don't choose to purchase a dedicated yoga strap to begin with, you can use a tie. Go ahead and choose the one that you have been trying to get rid of since your husband wore it back in '95 to your cousin's wedding. What better way to assure its retirement? Make sure whatever you use is made of a strong enough material to support your pushing and pulling on it a bit.

Setting Your Intent and Attitude

If you're thinking about practicing Holy Yoga, I imagine you already have the right attitude and intent. You're excited to start spending time worshiping the Lord and listening for His voice, while bringing improved health to your body—right? I'm just going to mention a couple more things about your mental outlook. I hope this helps you to weather any hurdles and stick with it, even when you sometimes want to quit.

Be Committed

As a discipline, Holy Yoga is not always easy. A spirit of faithfulness toward your practice will go a long way toward helping you persevere when you're too tired or just not in the mood. Make a promise to yourself at the outset that specifies the number of days per week you will practice and a time of day you will practice, and try to hold yourself to that promise. Yoga takes some getting used to. You most likely will not enjoy your first three or four sessions the way you will later. I am always up-front with my students in telling them that loving yoga takes time. The good news is that in Holy Yoga, at least we have the benefit of loving the time with the Lord right away! Stick with it.

Develop a Habit

Like anything new, Holy Yoga works best when done regularly, even if only for a few minutes at a time. It usually takes a month or more of repeating a behavior for it to become a habit, so give yourself time. I have read numerous studies relating to the length of time it takes to make or break a habit, and I've heard twenty-one days is key. I'm not sure how scientific it is, or if the study takes into account God's strength, but I do know the strength of God is never found lacking. If you have trouble during that first month and want to quit, pray for God's leading, ask for His strength and support, and try to discipline yourself to show up at your yoga spot at the specified time. Even if all you do is sit there cross-legged and pray or read the Bible, it helps you build and maintain your habit—and it certainly will not hurt! God will meet you whether you are in Downward Facing Dog—or if you're found lying down on your mat next to your dog!

Avoid a Competitive Spirit

If you're practicing at home, it shouldn't be too difficult to prevent the attitude of competition just as long as you do not set yourself up in the sight line of a mirror. You may feel you're competing with photos, videos, or even yourself. You are not competing! Your job is to love the Lord, listen to His voice, and listen to the needs and responses of your body. Your practice of Holy Yoga is between you and God—no one else.

Along with this idea, please remember not to judge yourself. This is not about performance. It's about bringing unity between your mind, body, and spirit and between you and God. That's all that matters.

A Few Physical Guidelines

If you're familiar with other sports and types of exercise but haven't practiced yoga, then this style of using your body, mind, and spirit together is going to feel unfamiliar and uncomfortable at first. It's so unlike every other type of sport. It doesn't involve speed, impact, competition, or any kind of "no pain, no gain" philosophy. In fact, while practicing yoga, I want you to listen to your body and avoid pain! I am always reminding my students to *do less and be more*. Here are a few other principles for a safe and fulfilling Holy Yoga practice.

Warm Up and Set Your Focus

One way in which yoga is the same as other kinds of exercise is that we always start slowly to warm up the body. In Holy Yoga, this is the time in which we set our intention. We pray and turn our hearts toward God, asking Him to inhabit our bodies, minds, and souls during this time. We use slow, easy stretches to get the body ready for more intense exercise. This warm-up period and the cooling down time at the end of practice are just as vital as the poses in-between, so don't give them short shrift.

Give Yourself Time to Learn

During your first few weeks of practice, remind yourself that you're still learning. Give yourself extra time to learn each pose. A regular routine will take you longer the first few times, so if necessary, do fewer postures at each session. You will begin to benefit from Holy Yoga right away, even going slowly and doing only a few postures each time.

Keep Your Movements Slow and Mindful

Even when you become a seasoned veteran of Holy Yoga, slow and mindful movements are key! While you may have heard of "power" yoga classes in which students rapidly perform moves and the emphasis is on working up a good sweat, that's not what I teach in Holy Yoga. Keep it slow. If you have less time, do fewer postures rather than trying to rush through a greater number of them. It is better to do one poses slowly and gently for five minutes than to power through ten poses in ten minutes, which does you no good at all.

No Pretzels!

Our goal is not to tie ourselves up in knots or imitate those exotic postures you may have seen in magazines. The postures you'll be learning are just as effective and much safer than the pretzels.

Remember Your Breathing

Yoga breathing accompanies movement at all times. You will be given direction on how to breathe in each pose. In general, we tend to inhale when the posture opens up the body and exhale when the posture folds the body. It might seem strange and foreign to begin with, but you'll get the hang of it as you continue to practice. As you breathe, you will create space in the body into which you can then move. Be conscious of the space that you are creating.

Function Over Form

Listen to your body. Go as far as you comfortably can in each stretch. You want to push slightly beyond your limit, but only gently. Never force your body into a position that causes pain. By paying attention to your body's signals, you will be emphasizing the function of the posture rather than trying to imitate an ideal form. When you honor the process, you honor yourself. The gift is in the process, not the arrival.

Always Do Both Sides of the Body

Whenever you do a movement on one side of the body, make sure you do it on the other side as well. Yoga is an incredible tool for balancing the body and bringing back symmetry where the strains of daily life may have gotten you out of alignment. To get the benefit of yoga's balancing effects, your practice should be balanced.

Stick to Routines, but Vary Them

Putting together a routine on your own is *not* a good idea initially. Yoga teachers carefully design the sequencing in each routine so that the body is not overly strained. Postures are arranged to warm you up, maximize the benefits of the main poses, keep the body in balance, and then cool you down.

As a beginner, please stick to the routines you find in this book or from other qualified yoga teachers, but don't do the same routine every time. As you cultivate a more regular practice, becoming more familiar with the poses and your body's capability, you can begin to make modifications to the routines to best suit your particular needs for each day.

Ready to Get to Work?

You've made it through all the introductory discussion, instructions, and guidelines. Don't be afraid to refer back to this chapter even as your practice of Holy Yoga progresses. It contains some good reminders that all yoga practitioners need to remember.

In the next chapter you're going to get to work on the first element of Holy Yoga—the breath. Let's go!

CHAPTER 8

The Breath of Life

Let everything that has breath praise the LORD.
Psalm 150:6

One of my favorite passages of Scripture is in the second chapter of Genesis: "The LORD God formed the man from the dust of the ground and *breathed into his nostrils the breath of life,* and the man became a living being" (v. 7, italics mine). Can you imagine the scene? There was God, down on the ground, getting His hands dirty. He gathered the dust and patted, molded, and sculpted until finally He was satisfied with His masterpiece. There was Adam, perfectly formed in His image. Imagine the look on God's face as He sat back and beheld his magnum opus—the pinnacle of his creation: a man.

But the man was not yet alive. He lay there—rigid, pale, unmoving. So God leaned over the body of Adam and blew His *very own life* into the man. That's what made Adam a living being, according to Genesis 2:7: *God's own breath.*

Can you envision Adam's coming to life? With oxygen in his lungs, his chest began to rise and fall, and he started to shift. His heart pumped blood and his skin developed a healthy color. His features filled out and his limbs stretched and he opened his eyes—only to look straight into the smiling face of God.

What a moment!

Imagining that scene helps me to comprehend the infinite importance of the breath. Every breath keeps us alive . . . and every breath we take is a direct gift from our Creator. As I picture Adam's chest, face, arms, and legs filling with oxygen, I appreciate the incredible power of the breath God gives me to keep every inch of my body healthy and working at its optimal level.

Because of its vast impact on the mind and body, mindful breathing has always been the very first discipline in the practice of yoga. And because we recognize the breath as the very essence of life God has granted us, in Holy Yoga we begin with the breath as well.

A Bit About Normal Breathing

Both ancient traditions and modern research confirm the intimate relationship between our breathing patterns and our health—physical, emotional, mental, and spiritual. Healthy respiration supports our overall well-being and is vital to reducing the effects of stress.

Each time we inhale, we bring fresh oxygen (the good stuff) into our body, which fills the blood and sets off the transformation of nutrients into fuel. When we exhale, we release carbon dioxide and toxins (the bad stuff) to be eliminated from the body. Not only is this the way God designed our bodies to work physically, it makes a wonderful metaphor for our practice of Holy Yoga breathing. The simplest way to begin training yourself to breathe mindfully is to sit quietly, focus on your breath, and imagine you are *breathing in* the goodness and grace of God and *breathing out* every negative thought and emotion.

In normal breathing conditions, our respiration is slow and regulated. During times of stress the breath becomes quick and shallow while the muscles tighten up. The circulation of blood is restricted and the body's organs suffer from diminished oxygen supply. Many of us live our lives in a state of nearly constant heightened stress levels, depriving our bodies for long periods of time of the oxygen they need for optimum health. Mindful breathing techniques can help us to restore healthier patterns of respiration while allowing us to de-stress and focus the energy of every breath on the Lord.

Holy Yoga Breathing Techniques

The breathing techniques I'm going to outline here are just a tiny taste of the numerous styles that have been developed by yoga practitioners over thousands of years. They are all fairly simple, so you may want to try all of them, just to get a feel for how they affect your body and spirit.

I believe yoga breathing techniques can be wonderful tools to help us focus in prayer. Part of Holy Yoga is simply learning to focus the breath in prayer, without even going into the postures. Take some time to practice these breathing exercises and choose the ones that work best for you. You will then have them at your disposal for private prayer times when you want to increase your calm and focus, as well as for times of stress when you need to consciously breathe in the beauty and goodness of God to soothe your spirit.

Focused Breathing

If you are new to yoga, this simple technique will be the one you utilize as you begin to practice the postures explained later in the book. This is also an excellent tool for use during meditation and prayer. You may want to bring a specific prayer with you into this exercise, or focus on God Himself.

1. Sit comfortably and check your posture. Bring your back up straight and place your hands on your knees. (You can be sitting on the floor, on a bed, or on a chair.) Close your eyes.

2. Breathe normally for a few cycles, observing your breath. Breathe only through your nose unless you have an obstruction.

3. Slowly begin to take your breath in control. Make your breath a little deeper, a little longer. On exhalation, make the effort to expel every last bit of air from your lungs before starting a new breath. At this point, keep your focus on your breath.

4. Begin allowing a brief pause at the top of the inhalation, as well as after you exhale. Notice how your body moves with your breath, and begin to consciously allow your body the freedom to move exactly the way it wants to with your breath. Allow your entire abdomen to expand and your chest to rise.

5. Now you may want to add a conscious prayer to your breath. For example, upon inhale, slowly say the words in your mind, "Lord Jesus Christ." Upon exhale: "Have mercy on me." Keep your focus on the rhythm of your breath and your prayer. When your mind starts to wander, gently bring it back, first to your breath and then to your prayer.

6. After about 5 minutes of focused breathing, let go of the conscious control of your breath. Release it to God, thanking Him for the gift of your breath. Sit quietly, breathing normally, for a few minutes. Notice how your energy, your thoughts, and your feelings have changed through this brief exercise.

Belly Breathing

Belly Breathing is very similar to Focused Breathing, but it requires a slightly different focus. You will be learning to expand your belly while breathing—something that seems very unnatural to those of us accustomed to sucking in our bellies all the time! But breathing with the full use of the belly is the most natural way to breathe, as you will notice if you ever watch a newborn baby. When a baby breathes, his or her little tummy fills up with air and completely expands. Lucky babies—they're not self-conscious about their waistlines and could care less if they have to bump up to a Pampers #4!

Again, in our heightened state of stress we tend to have very shallow breathing habits. In fact, it is estimated that we often use only the top 25 percent of our lungs. Breathing into the belly allows for intentional oxygenation and replenishing of all the systems of the body to aid in their health.

With this exercise, Psalm 16:11 is fitting. Upon inhale: "You will fill me," and upon exhale, "with joy in your presence." If you like you can make it into a direct prayer by saying, "Lord, fill me..." (This is a wonderful way to pray Scripture throughout your practice of Holy Yoga.)

1. Begin the same as you did with Focused Breathing. Take a few slow, conscious breaths, inhaling and exhaling deeply, with a small pause in between.
2. When you are ready, begin to imagine that your waist is wrapped in an elastic band that extends from your hipbones up to the bottom of your ribcage. On your next breath, expand your belly in all directions, front, sides, and back, pushing that elastic band out as far as it will go. Try to keep your chest from expanding.
3. Exhale and contract the abdomen.
4. Repeat for about 5 minutes, keeping your focus on your breath and your prayer.

Retained Breath Exercise

This is a helpful way to slow down your breathing even further and provide the optimum supply of oxygen to your body. It has been shown to increase oxygenation of the blood as well as strengthen the lungs.

You may want to recite a short passage of Scripture during this exercise, no more than a few words. Try Psalm 104:33: "I will sing praise to my God as long as I live."

1. Sit up straight.
2. Inhale for 4 seconds while mentally reciting your brief prayer. As you inhale, first push your belly forward, then push out your ribs and allow your chest to rise.
3. Hold your breath for 16 seconds. If you don't want to watch the clock, simply recite the verse 4 times in your mind. If you find this length of breath-holding difficult at the start, just hold for 8 seconds, and gradually build up to 16 seconds.
4. Exhale for 8 seconds, reciting the verse twice. For the first 6 seconds, just allow your collar bone and ribs to relax, so the breath goes out automatically. For the last 2 seconds push your stomach in gently to expel the air from your lungs.

Cleansing Breath/Breath of Fire

The Cleansing Breath is helpful if we have mucus in the air passages or blockages in the chest. In this practice we deliberately breathe faster and use only the abdomen, not the chest. The breath is short, rapid, and strong. You use the lungs as a pump, creating pressure as they expel the air to help clear the rubbish from the air passages. This is a good exercise for when you feel heavy or foggy in the head because of its energizing effect. Don't practice this at night before bed—it really can keep you awake!

Caution: Be careful with this technique. You may become dizzy, so conclude this practice with some slow breaths, and rest for a few moments before returning to normal activity.

Because of the rapidity of this exercise, you probably will not want to use a Scripture passage but simply focus on the energizing presence of God.

1. Sit up tall, or stand comfortably with your arms at your sides. Take a few slow, deep breaths.

2. When you are ready, take a slow deep breath and then do 15 to 20 fast exhalations through your nose, each followed by a quick (half-second) inhale.

3. Repeat this only twice. Conclude by taking a few more slow, deep breaths, and thank God for the gift of life.

Alternate Nostril Breathing

I don't know about you, but I don't think much about my nose unless it's stuffy or giving me problems—in which case I get very annoyed with my nose. I suppose if you had asked me, I would have assumed that we breathe evenly through both of our nostrils most of the time. But I would have been wrong!

In normal breathing, a healthy person breathes through both nostrils, but the emphasis alternates between the two nostrils in cycles of about two hours. But since most of us are not in optimum health, our cycles are not balanced, which leads to other imbalances in our system.

Alternate Nostril Breathing (ANB) helps to create balance and harmony in the body by giving each nostril equal time. It can also help to strengthen the weaker nostril. There are several different types of ANB exercises, and this is one of the simpler ones suitable for beginners. Any brief Scripture or prayer may be used.

Please note: Alternate Nostril Breathing should not be used if you have a stuffy nose or your nasal passages are blocked in any way, or without first discussing it with your medical advisor. Under no circumstances should anything be forced—an important rule throughout your yoga practice!

1. Sit comfortably, with your back up straight. To position your hand for closing off the nostrils: hold up your right hand with your palm toward you, extend your thumb

upward and your last 2 fingers straight out. Fold down
your index and middle fingers.

2. Place your thumb against the right side of your nose, closing
   off your right nostril. Inhale slowly for 4 seconds.

3. Pause the breath. Release your thumb from your nose, and
   simultaneously place the last 2 fingers of your right hand
   on the side of your left nostril, closing it off.

4. Exhale for 4 seconds. Without changing your finger
   position, inhale for 4 seconds.

5. Pause. Release the left nostril and close off the right and
   exhale.

6. Repeat for 3 or 4 cycles.

Victorious Breath

The "*Victorious*" breath is the most commonly used breath in
a physical yoga practice. It is used during the practice of poses and
routines to regulate the flow of oxygen to the body. You will hear the
sound of the *victorious* breath in almost any yoga class anywhere.
It is created by toning the epiglottis to intentionally create a sound
at the back of your throat. The sound is often compared to the
whispered sound of "*haaaa*" in the back of your throat as you
breathe. It creates direct audible feedback to you so that you can
be aware of the state of how your body in using the breath. The
quality of your breath is directly related to your state of mind, so
by becoming aware of your breath you become mindful of yourself
in the pose. Generally you inhale and exhale faster at the beginning
of a breath cycle, and your breath begins to taper off at the end.
With the *victorious* breath, try and keep the same rate of breath
flowing at all times, from start to finish. The *victorious* breath is
your practice breath, the one you will use during the poses.

1. Take a deep, full inhale followed by a deep exhalation.

2. Inhale through your nose while you slightly constrict the
   muscles in the back of the throat to create a whispering sound.

3. Exhale through your nose to create the same sound.
4. Keep the flow of your breath even and smooth from the beginning to the end of each inhalation-exhalation cycle.
5. Continue the breath during the entirety of your posture practice.

Breath and Prayer

These breathing exercises on their own are a wonderful means of keeping our minds and bodies calm during prayer. If you are going to spend some time praying or reading the Word, you can start with five minutes practicing one of these breathing techniques to center and calm yourself and set your focus. Here are a few of my favorite verses to open up my devotional time or start my day:

- I praise you because I am fearfully and wonderfully made. (Psalm 139:14)
- Open my eyes that I may see wonderful things in your law. (Psalm 119:18)
- I can do everything through him who gives me strength. (Philippians 4:13)
- Praise be to the God and Father of our Lord Jesus Christ. (Ephesians 1:3)
- Let us continually offer to God a sacrifice of praise. (Hebrews 13:15)
- Hallelujah! For our Lord God Almighty reigns. (Revelation 19:6)
- Everything is possible for him who believes. (Mark 9:23)

Now that you're familiar with the way the breath can soothe your spirit and be a means of prayer in itself, you may find yourself wanting to go a bit further down this path. It's time to take a look at the second major facet of Holy Yoga: meditation.

CHAPTER 9

Meditation: Be Still and Know

Within your temple, O God, we meditate on your unfailing love.
Psalm 48:9

I am so excited to talk with you about meditation. As much as I love practicing the postures of Holy Yoga and worshiping God with my entire body and soul, the quiet communion with God during meditation has come to be my favorite part of the day. These are the moments I feel closest to Him, when I often hear His voice speaking clearly in my heart. Meditation is one of the greatest treasures God has granted us!

I am going to give you a brief introduction to the idea of Christian meditation, and I trust it's enough to get you started. If you wish to explore the topic in more depth, countless books and articles are available to take you further on your journey. In any case, no one can really teach you to meditate, especially not in a book. The way to learn is to do it. This chapter will provide a few guidelines and techniques, but you will discover for yourself how to meditate as you allow God to be your guide and discipline yourself to practice.

Biblical References to Meditation

Meditation is an ancient discipline that God's people have practiced throughout recorded history. All you have to do is use a concordance to find numerous uses of the words "meditate" and "meditation" in the Bible. In fact, the very first book of the Bible records Isaac, Abraham's son, doing this: "He went out to the field one evening to meditate" (Gen. 24:63).

You'll find most references to meditation in the Psalms, such 19:14: "May my words and my thoughts be acceptable to you, O LORD, my refuge and my redeemer!" (TEV). I particularly like Psalm 119:99, which says, "I understand more than all my teachers, because I meditate on your instructions" (TEV). It sounds kind of arrogant! But the truth is that meditation leads to deeper understanding of God's truth because it is a way of interacting directly with God and His Word and allowing Him to speak straight into your heart.

What Is Christian Meditation?

Just a few years ago, I wasn't even aware that Christians could meditate. Like most people, I had heard of meditation associated with Eastern religions and New Age and secular concepts such as TM (transcendental meditation). But I thought it was off-limits to Jesus-followers.

Luckily, I was wrong. Like all of yoga, the practice of meditation is a gift of God that others have co-opted for their uses and to suit their own ends. When used in the service of God, it is a discipline that puts us squarely into the place where He can work in us.

We Westerners are familiar with prayer as a verbal communication with God. Meditation is an exercise in contemplation. It is a silent or contemplative form of prayer in which we focus on God, a specific attribute of God, or a passage of Scripture. We think, pray, then allow our hearts and minds to be open to hearing God's voice in the silence. I see meditation as an immeasurably valuable way to deepen my relationship with God and find pure joy and contentment in my communion with Him.

Sometimes it's difficult for Christians to see how meditation can really be prayer. After all, it's so . . . *silent*. But as Hank Hanegraaff says,

> Think for a moment about your prayer life. Could it be that it is characterized by constant babbling? Might it be that even the chatter of your mind is deafening? Could it be that your shallow askings drown out the sound of the very One whose voice you so long to hear? Have you ever considered how glorious the sounds of silence might be?[1]

One of the reasons we meditate is to create silence so that we can hear that Voice.

We have to be careful to avoid a works-based philosophy when practicing meditation. We do not draw closer to God through our own efforts, but by the saving grace of Jesus Christ. Still, we can put ourselves in a position for the Lord to do this work in us. Meditation acts as an invitation to which the Holy Spirit responds, enters in, and accomplishes the work of God in us.[2]

We've discussed earlier in this book the differences between Eastern types of yoga and Holy Yoga. The similarities and differences hold true for meditation as well. While Eastern meditation is about emptying and detachment, Christian meditation is about emptying the parts of self that are littered with worldliness to make room for our Creator; detaching from the craziness of life in order to find a deeper attachment to God. It's about our growth in Christ and our spiritual formation, which is a work of the Lord— we cannot do it on our own. Paul said in his letter to the Philippians, "He who began a good work in you will carry it on to completion until the day of Christ Jesus" (1:6). The Lord is working in us, so we need to continually put ourselves in positions to be molded and refined and to hear His voice.

I love this passage from *Of the Imitation of Christ* by Thomas à Kempis: "Blessed are they that enter far into inward things, and endeavor to prepare themselves more and more, by daily exercises, for the receiving of Heavenly secrets."[3] Christian meditation does indeed prepare us for hearing the whisperings of God—the heavenly secrets. I can hardly imagine a sweeter blessing!

And just what are those heavenly secrets? Often meditation leads to insights, but not always what you might think. You may be expecting deep spiritual wisdom and instead receive an understanding of how to handle a situation you're facing in your marriage. A friend of mine received amazingly detailed guidance on whether to take a job she had been offered and exactly how to handle it. God meets us where we are—and where we are is often mired in the humdrum details of everyday life. Yet unbelievably, those details are part and parcel of the heavenly secrets.

In order to persist in meditation, we have to *desire* to be with God and to hear His voice. That's a big challenge for most of us. I often *want* the desire to hear God's voice, but I don't actually *have* the desire. I might rather be doing something—anything—else. That's where prayer comes in. We pray for the desire to commune with God and for the discipline to put ourselves in the place where that can happen. It's a vital part of committing to the discipline of meditation.

While I'm on the topic of our need to pray *about* our meditation, I need to mention that we should also pray for *protection* each time we meditate. We are entering the spiritual realm, and we're wise to tread carefully. We want to be open to God's voice and His alone. We simply ask God to lay His hand of protection upon us, building hedges of shelter around us, and surrounding us with His light as He ministers to our spirits.[4]

There is so much information available about why to meditate. The single reason that propels me is that I desire to give God all of my attention, to be in His Word, and to rest in the peace that only

He can give. There are many days in meditation that I don't come away with anything that feels like a special insight or revelation. It doesn't matter. I gave God my attention, and He gave me His. We rested in each other's presence—and as much as I enjoyed it, I suspect He may have enjoyed it even more.

To meditate is to spend time quietly devoted to God, listening for His voice, yet being content even in not hearing it. In meditation we are seeking not to know more *about* God but to know God directly.[5] If we are unwilling to take the time to listen as God prompts us and provides us with peace and clarity, we will exist in a constant space of asking, of seeking and never finding.

In Holy Yoga, we normally have a meditation period after we have practiced our postures for the day and are relaxed and focused. In a group setting, this is usually only a period of a few minutes that is quite beneficial, but at home you can take as long as you like. You may also want to set aside time for meditation several times a week apart from your practice of yoga postures.

If you desire to meditate at the end of your yoga practice, you might want to decide beforehand if there is a particular passage of Scripture or attribute of God you want to have as the focus for your meditation. You can either memorize it, write it down and have it with you, or begin your yoga practice with your Bible open next to you so that it's handy when you need it. You may also decide to simply listen to God in silence, using your mindful breathing to help keep you focused . . . and awake!

Keeping Distractions at Bay

The most common frustration while meditating is the way our minds wander. Especially when you begin, you'll notice that you may not even be able to focus on God and your breath for five seconds without a stray thought creeping in. This is normal! It's part of the discipline of learning to quiet your mind.

When distractions occur or your mind wanders, just gently bring it back to your focus. Avoid chastising yourself or becoming frustrated. As often as you need to, reset your focus and continue on.

The breath is a helpful tool for dealing with distractions. You can bring your mind back from its bunny trails by inhaling God's peace and light and love and exhaling the distracting thought that is plaguing you. Simply give the thought up to God.

Many people find visualizations to be helpful in keeping distractions at bay. This simply means holding a picture of something in your mind to help keep your thoughts from straying too wildly. Some people like to envision an idyllic scene like a Hawaiian sunset or a snow-topped mountain. Others prefer to hold in mind a picture of the cross or of Jesus. Some use symbols such as a candle. The idea is to hold that visual in your mind as a point of focus to which you can bring back your attention when your thoughts have wandered.

Recently I was in a group yoga class and had a wonderful meditation experience. I felt great and didn't want to get up from my mat even though the class was dispersing. When I opened my eyes, a woman was staring at me. I felt so self-conscious! But she told me she was fascinated with how I had been so deep into the meditation and looked so serene and content. What was my secret? she wondered. She thought I must have been visualizing a lovely tropical island or some similar romantic place.

Talk about embarrassed! I had to tell this woman that, no, I wasn't on a tropical island. In fact, in my visualization I had been sitting at home in my closet! Yes, right there on the floor, with the shoes all around me and the clothes hanging over me. As a mother of three amazing kiddos, I need my designated *Do Not Enter or Else* space. That's my closet. It's where I cry, where I pray, and where God has met me in times of deepest despair and joy. It's my "grace place," as I call it. So you see, you can use visualization however you like, as long as it works to help keep you focused.

Whatever means you use to manage the wanderings of your mind, remember that your goal is to keep your entire heart, soul, mind, and strength focused on "the glory of God in the face of Christ" (2 Cor. 4:6).[6]

Tips on Technique

1. Find a quiet place where you won't be disturbed or interrupted. For most of us, this can be the most difficult part of meditation.
2. Precede your meditation with some yoga postures if you like.
3. Sitting upright is the preferred pose, because it is important to have your head, neck, and trunk in a straight line to enhance energy flow and proper breathing. Lying down can work only if you don't fall asleep. If you are sitting, it helps to have a small cushion under the sitting bones as this will help to keep your posture erect.
4. Bring your attention away from external activities and bring your focus to your breath. Breathe in and out slowly, using the Focused Breathing explained in chapter 8. If you intend to meditate on a Scripture, begin to read it or recite it. When other thoughts come into your head, gently let them go by and draw your attention back.
5. At this point, you may feel yourself quieting more and more deeply. I liken this feeling to listening to someone who is whispering very quietly—you must be very still to hear. That someone is God.

As you begin a practice, the most important thing is to be sure that the process is enjoyable so that you will want to return to it again and again. Five to ten minutes in the beginning is plenty; anything over fifteen to twenty is likely to be counterproductive, but be your own judge.

Scripture Meditation

You may decide you'd like to try a type of Christian meditation that's a bit more structured and based on passages of Scripture. There is an ancient form of meditation called *lectio divina* that people have practiced for centuries, and it has recently enjoyed a resurgence in popularity across Christian denominations. The meditation I'm outlining here is loosely based on traditional *lectio divina* and should be practiced when you'd like to spend at least thirty to sixty minutes in uninterrupted meditation.

Get Quiet and Pray

First, choose the passage on which you'd like to meditate. It could be one or two verses, but no more than ten. Settle yourself in a quiet place with your Bible, study materials if you have them, your journal, and a pen. Make sure you won't be disturbed, and that you are comfortable. Pray that you will have God's leading in this process and that you will be open to His voice.

Study

Read the passage you've selected. Make sure you understand it. Read the surrounding verses if you need to, or the notes in your Bible or any other commentary you have available. If you own different translations of the Bible, such as the King James, the Amplified, and the NIV, read the passage in multiple versions to aid your understanding. Ask yourself questions such as, *Who was speaking? What was the historical context? What did they mean at the time? Is that meaning the same today?* Psalm 119:27 says, "Let me understand the teaching of your precepts; then I will meditate on your wonders." The principle is that *first* we learn and appreciate the passage, then we meditate on it.

Muse

Once you are comfortable with your understanding of the passage, begin to ponder it. Turn it over in your mind, looking at it from different angles. See if your perspective on this passage is enlarged or enhanced. One way to do this is to take a brief verse and emphasize different words each time you say it. For example, Matthew 28:20: "I am with you always."

I am with you always.
I *am* with you always.
I am *with* you always.
I am with *you* always.
I am with you *always*.

It can be enlightening to see just how many meanings we can glean from just a few words!

Respond

Now allow yourself to personally interact with the passage. Ask yourself, *How does this touch me today? What words stand out to me? What emotions does this passage elicit in me? How does it enlarge my understanding of God or my relationship to Him? Does this passage motivate me to any type of action in my life?* Jot down in your journal anything that comes to you. Try not to direct your own thinking but allow the Spirit to lead you.

Pray

Now, pray the passage aloud. Speak God's Words back to Him. Continue praying through the passage and allowing God to speak to you as long as you feel led. Leave room for silence in which you simply sit still and know that He is God.

Rest

Last, rest for a bit. Enjoy God's presence. Don't think too hard—just experience God's love and His message to you if He has one. Now is a good time to make notes about your experience in your journal.

Meditation as a Discipline

If meditation is still sounding a bit vague, I understand. On paper, it really is hard to explain. But I guarantee that if you give it a sincere try, you'll begin to understand how it works. It can be challenging, but the rewards of meditation are great. If you commit to meditation perhaps two or three times a week for a month, you might be surprised at the profound impact it has on your spiritual life.

At the very least, your spirit will benefit from intentional moments of quietness. We all need a break from the rush-rush-rush of daily life! I tend to agree with psychiatrist C. G. Jung, who once said, "Hurry is not *of* the Devil; it *is* the Devil."[7]

Meditation is not just a fringe aspect of Christianity—it is at the heart of our faith. Isn't it true that the center of the Christian life is a personal relationship with Jesus Christ? No matter how unfamiliar the concept remains in today's church, taking time to commune intimately with God leads to the reward that is the most precious gift of all—greater intimacy with your heavenly Father.

PART THREE

The Postures

CHAPTER 10

Putting It All Together

At the name of Jesus every knee should bow, in heaven
and on earth and under the earth.
Philippians 2:10

Y ou are finally ready to begin practicing Holy Yoga! In the
remainder of the book, I will teach you a sampling of different types of yoga postures. Chapter 20 gives suggested routines—
the order in which I recommend you practice the postures.

For your first week of practice, I suggest you set aside about five
to ten minutes each day to practice the breathing exercises from
chapter 8. Then you may want to move into posture practice by
scheduling time periods of about thirty minutes each, several times
a week, to begin learning the poses. At the end of your posture practice is a great time to practice meditation. Of course, you will find
what works for you. The important thing is to be proactive about
getting Holy Yoga into your schedule—even write it on your cal-
endar! This is crucial for establishing a new discipline in your life.

As Christians we often talk about our daily "quiet time." We
know we're supposed to be spending time with the Lord—reading
Scripture, studying, and praying—but sometimes we lose our
excitement and find it difficult to keep up the habit. Holy Yoga can
be instrumental in restoring a regular devotional time to your life!
You can use any combination of Bible reading, prayer, mindful
breathing, meditation, and postures. You can focus on a passage of

Scripture, bring personal issues before the Lord, or simply come to His feet open to whatever the time brings. The idea of Holy Yoga, as you know by now, is simply to come before Him in praise and worship, with a quiet enough mind that you can hear Him speak.

Please go easy on yourself. If you're practicing Holy Yoga for the first time, again, it will feel unfamiliar and there will be times you may be frustrated or impatient. Give those feelings up to God, and return your focus to Him. You will find that you continually need to reset your intent. The temptation is always to return to thoughts of self, or worldly issues pressing in on you. Gently keep pulling your focus back to the face of Jesus.

A Few Definitions

You may want to briefly skim through this section to familiarize yourself with some terms I will use later in the descriptions of the postures. Later you can refer back to it, if you need to recall a certain term.

(In alphabetical order)

Active. Intentional use of your muscles and/or energy.

Child's Pose. This posture, in which you are face-down on the floor with your knees up under you, will be explained later but I wanted to mention that it's a wonderful resting as well as worship pose. When I am in Child's Pose on the floor, it reminds me that I am floored by God's awesome majesty, and it is my honor to be laid out for Him. As I rest in Child's Pose, I also envision that God my Father is holding me, nurturing me, and cradling me in a very safe space. This posture can be used on its own for prayer or meditation.

Constant adjustments with the breath. The breath is an indicator of what is going on in the physical realm. When your breath is labored because of a strenuous posture, try to stabilize it by gently easing out of the pose and find rest *in and at the edge* of your comfort zone. Your growth lies in the acceptance of where you are without condemnation or needing to be more.

Corpse Pose. So-called because it consists of lying flat on your back and being still and quiet. We usually finish our practice in Corpse Pose, resting contentedly in God's grace. It can be the hardest part of our practice, as it calls us to simply "be" before the Lord, so that He can speak to us if He so desires.

Crown. This refers to the very top of the head.

Drop your knees. This is a usual directive to make a pose gentle and/or to take pressure off of the lower back. It simply means to bend your knees as much as you need to in order to be comfortable in the pose.

Energetically. Imagine squeezing your muscles to your bones, becoming aware of how the energy in those muscles is active or passive.

Engaged. Active and deliberate use of energy in relation to muscles.

Four corners of the feet. The four points of the sole of the foot: two on the ball of the foot and two on the heel.

Great toe. The big toe(s).

Heels of the hands. The fleshy part of the palm between the base thumb joint and the base pinky joint, just below the center of the palm.

Inner eyes of the elbows. Inside edges of the elbow joints.

Inner rotation. Usually mentioned in relation to the thighs, it occurs when the designated part of the body comes toward the midline.

Isometric ally. A muscular contraction against energetic resistance where the length of the muscle remains the same. It is the idea of energetic engagement and resistance without actual movement.

Micro movements. The idea of making continual small movements in an effort to deepen physical and emotional awareness.

Midline. The center of the body in relation to the spine and core.

Natural curves. The natural physical design of curves in the neck and lower back

Outer rotation. Usually mentioned in relation to the thighs, it is when the designated part of the body moves away from the midline.

Pads of the fingertips. The fleshy part of the fingertips.

Praise Feet. Open the soles of your feet so that they, along with all 10 toes, are outstretched, as though they were in worship. Allow all the tips of your toes to radiate away from the ball of your foot. This is no flexing of the feet.

Praise Hands. Open your hands so that your palm and all 5 fingers are outstretched, like in worship. Allow all your fingertips to radiate energetically outward.

Props. Block, bolster, mat, strap (explained in chapter 7).

Rooted. Consciously connecting and finding a physical center.

Shoulder Draw. As you sit or stand tall, drop the tops of your shoulders away from your ears and lift the top of your crown upward toward the heavens, lengthening the spine as much as possible. Next draw the shoulder blades back by broadening the front side of the chest. Imagine the shoulder blades coming together so much so that you could hold a penny between your shoulder blades. Keeping that engagement, drop the bottom of the shoulder blades toward the tail, accentuating the upward lift of the crown.

Side body. The space between the shoulders and the hips, along the length of the body.

Skull Draw. As you sit or stand tall, gently retract the skull so that the back of the head moves toward the wall behind you, only an inch or so. Stop where it feels most comfortable. Allow it to be natural. When you get to that space of slight and natural resistance, drop your shoulders away from the ears. A "skull draw" is essential for maintaining and protecting the natural curve in the neck. It enables us to maintain alignment of the entire spine when we take our gaze upward, avoiding potential injury. Once you draw back, try to relax your face and jaw, softening the tongue and the gaze.

Squeezing. Engaging or flexing.

Table Top. The pose in which you are on all fours.

Standing Postures

I look up to the mountains; does my strength come from
mountains? No, my strength comes from GOD who made heaven,
and earth, and mountains. He won't let you stumble,
your Guardian God won't fall asleep.
Psalm 121:1–3 (The Message)

S tanding poses are the most essential and foundational of all
poses because they lay the groundwork for more advanced
postures. They teach the principles of alignment and engagement
while building power, stability, and strength. In addition to
producing stamina in the legs, standing postures also assist in
effective circulation, digestion, mobility, balance, and physical
awareness.

When you are practicing a standing series, the heart and
lungs are detoxing the blood and insulating the nervous system,
leaving you feeling fresh, attentive, renewed, and settled. All of the
directives given are to inspire a deeper experience of the pose.

Please take responsibility for yourself while practicing these
poses. Honor when it is time to move forward and when it is time
to rest. Holy Yoga is a practice that is unique to you and should
be done in the context of joy, worship, and praise. Make this your
own. Do what feels right and leave the rest alone.

As you move through these standing poses, imagine yourself
accentuating your foundation and strength in Christ. Push yourself
a bit. Trust that in Him there is the strength needed to become

fully present. Use the postures to manifest your strength for His glory. Keep reaching further, going deeper, and receiving more of the abundance we are promised in Him and that He is so eager for us to embrace.

Mountain Pose

This is the starting place for many standing postures.

1. Stand tall and lift the crown (top of the head) upward away from the ears.
2. Distribute the weight evenly over the four corners of each foot.
3. Engage (or flex) the legs and draw the shoulder blades onto the back body.

MOUNTAIN HANDS PRAYER

Tabletop (or Table) Pose

This is another common starting place for numerous postures.

1. Get down on all fours with arms straight but elbows *not* locked.
2. Hands should be directly under your shoulders, palms spread on the floor. Emphasize the length in the side body.
3. Knees should be directly under your hips.
4. Be sure the navel draws upward to counter the sway in the low back.

TABLETOP POSE

Downward Facing Dog Pose

1. Begin in Tabletop Pose. Inhale.
2. Exhaling, lift the hips up and back toward the ceiling while pressing into the mat through the palms. Engage the legs, moving your weight into the legs. Don't lock your knees. Press your heels toward the floor, but not all the way if it causes pain.
3. Drop the crown of the head toward the floor energetically while you lengthen the side body.
4. Return to Table Pose and repeat 1–3 times. On the last time, hold the pose for 6–8 breaths.

TIPS: Bring the shoulder blades behind the heart (on the back body). Soften the heart toward the thighs. Lift the inner thighs toward the back of the room. Lift your navel.

TABLETOP POSE   DOWNWARD FACING DOG 2

Extended Side-Angle Pose

1. Begin in Downward Facing Dog.
2. Bring the right foot forward next to the right hand. Make sure the right knee is bent 90 degrees. Spin the left foot, so that the outer edge of the left foot presses into the mat for stability.

3. Make sure that the front knee is over the 2nd and 3rd toe and that the kneecap is moving toward the pinky toe.

4. Bring the right hand inside or outside the right foot. Extend the left arm toward the ceiling, so that your left and right shoulders form a vertical line. Use a block to support your bottom hand if necessary, or bring the elbow to the front thigh.

5. Keep the back leg strong and the hip lifting. Bring your gaze up toward your right hand, and hold for 4–6 breaths.

6. Return to Downward Facing Dog and repeat other side.

TIPS: For an additional extension, bring the left bicep alongside the left ear. Make sure the extension is from the hip. Keep the chest open.

EXTENDED SIDE ANGLE 2

Triangle Pose

1. Start in Mountain Pose. Exhaling, step your right leg out to the side in a wide stance.

2. Inhale and raise your arms out to the side parallel to the floor. Keep your left foot pointing forward while turning

your right foot straight out to the right. Keep your hips facing front.

3. Exhale while reaching the right fingertips toward the right toes, and hinge at the hips toward the right, bringing the right hand to the top of the right thigh or shin. If you are more advanced, the hand can be on the floor.

4. Lift the left arm high and reach upward toward the ceiling.

5. Gaze upward at the hand, gaze neutral, or gaze at the floor. Hold for 4–6 breaths.

6. Return to Step 2 and repeat other side.

TIPS: Press through outer edge of the back foot, keeping that leg engaged. Crown moves toward the front of the room as the tail moves toward the back. Bring your top lung and hip back as you move your bottom lung and hip forward, essentially stacking the hips and lungs.

TRIANGLE   TRIANGLE 2

Revolved Triangle Pose

1. Start in Standing Forward Fold. Step your right leg back about 3 feet to a comfortable stride with both sets of toes facing forward.
2. Inhale and lengthen your spine. Place the right hand to the inside of the left foot on the floor or on a block.
3. Keeping the length in the spine, extend the left arm out and upward toward the sky, drawing the torso open. To make the position easier, soften your left knee, or move your right hand toward the right.
4. Hold for 3–4 breaths, then repeat other side.

TIPS: Root down through the front heel as you draw the front hip back and away from that heel. Lengthen the spine first by moving the crown forward and the tail back, then twist.

REVOLVED TRIANGLE

REVOLVED TRIANGLE 2

Warrior 1 Pose

1. Begin in Mountain Pose. Step the right foot straight out front in a comfortable stride, about 3 feet.
2. Turn the back heel in slightly so the foot is at approximately a 45-degree angle, pressing the outer edge of the back foot firmly into the mat.
3. Bend the front knee to a 90-degree angle, while slowly extending the arms forward and up overhead. Be sure the shoulders soften away from the ears.
4. Hold for 3–4 breaths. Return to Mountain Pose and repeat other side.

TIPS: The front knee should be over the 2nd and 3rd toe and moving outward toward the pinky toe. Keep the hips squared to the front of the room. Root the weight to the outer edge of the back foot, engaging the leg and upward/inward lifting through the back thigh. Slightly soften the tailbone toward the mat, and draw the navel in and up while extending upward through the crown. Be well rooted here, strong in your foundation but upward lifting in your awareness of Christ.

WARRIOR I

Warrior 2 Pose

1. Begin in Mountain Pose. Step the right foot out to the side so that your feet are a comfortable stride apart in distance. Keep your hips facing forward (to the side wall).
2. Turn the left heel in slightly so the foot is at an approximately 45-degree angle. Turn your right foot out so that your toes are pointing toward the right.
3. Bend the right knee to a 90-degree angle while lifting your arms straight out to the sides, parallel to the floor, palms down.
4. Imagine your fingertips intentionally reaching toward opposite ends of the room with as much intensity as possible.
5. Open your heart. Be intentional about receiving the abundance of His love and grace.
6. Repeat on other side.

TIPS: Keep the left leg engaged by pressing the weight to the outer edge of that foot. You know that your leg is engaged by lifting the kneecap and squeezing the muscle to the bone. As you root through the outer edge of the left foot, energetically lift the inner thigh up toward the pelvis. It is the practice of giving

WARRIOR 2   WARRIOR 2-2

and receiving. It teaches us to exert but be conscious enough to receive Him in every exertion or deed that we do. It calls us to be intentional and present.

Humble Warrior Pose

1. Begin in Warrior 1. Interlace your hands at your tailbone. Drop your knuckles toward the floor as if there were a 10-pound weight in your hands.
2. Take a little back bend here if you can: open the chest, drop the head back, and lift the chin upward.
3. Gently hinge forward from the hips, keeping the hands interlaced behind you. Rest your right shoulder on your right thigh. If you are more advanced, you can drop the right shoulder to the inside edge of the knee or thigh.
4. After a few breaths, come back up to Warrior 1. Repeat on other side.

TIPS: Bend into the front knee as much as you can, and then gently draw the front hip back and in toward the midline of the body. Keep the outer edge of the back foot rooting into the mat, lifting the inner arch and pressing the back hip forward. The key is to surrender and trust.

HUMBLE WARRIOR   HUMBLE WARRIOR 2

Crescent Lunge Pose

1. Begin in Downward Facing Dog.
2. Step the right foot forward and place it on the mat between your hands.
3. Stay on the ball of the left foot. You can drop the knee if necessary.
4. Lift your torso off your thigh so that it is vertical, bringing your shoulders directly over the hips.
5. Bring your arms up, biceps next to your ears, softening your shoulders away from your ears.
6. Hold for 2–3 breaths and release. Repeat other side.

TIPS: If you like, you can take a back bend here, gently dropping your head back and pressing your chest to the ceiling. You can interlace your fingers at your lower back or rest your hands on the front thigh.

CRESCENT LUNGE   CRESCENT LUNGE 2

Revolved Crescent Lunge Pose

1. Begin in Downward Facing Dog.
2. Step the right foot forward and place it on the mat between your hands.

3. Stay on the ball of the left foot. You can drop the knee if necessary.
4. Bring your left hand to the floor inside of the right foot.
5. Take your right hand upward, twisting the torso.
6. Bring your hands into prayer position and rotate for a deeper twist.
7. Hold for 2–3 breaths and release. Repeat other side.

CRESCENT LUNGE

REVOLVED CRESCENT 2

Chair Pose

1. Start in Mountain Pose.
2. Keeping your spine straight, bend your knees as close to 90 degrees as possible, as if you were sitting down in a chair. Allow your posterior to extend out toward the back (do not tuck it under). Touch your fingertips to the floor on either side of your feet if you can.

3. Reach your arms straight out front and then upward toward the sky, keeping them parallel to one another until your arms are alongside your ears. Drop your shoulders down.

4. Grow tall through the spine, all the while keeping the knees bent to 90 degrees.

5. Hold for 3–4 breaths, then release, drawing your hands to your heart center in prayer and returning to Mountain Pose.

6. Repeat 2–3 times.

TIPS: Keep your spine straight and lift your torso off of your thighs. Draw your thighs energetically toward one another as though there were an imaginary block between them. This is a wonderful posture of praise to our Father.

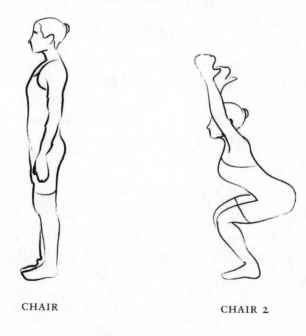

CHAIR   CHAIR 2

Standing Spread-Leg Pose

1. Begin in Mountain Pose. With your right foot, step out to the right in a nice wide stance, about the length of one leg. Keep your feet parallel, toes pointing forward.
2. Bringing your hands to your hips, extend the crown upward as to lengthen the spine.
3. Hinging from the hips with a straight spine, fold forward.
4. You can relax your hands where comfortable: on the floor with or without blocks, on the outer edges of your feet, or gripping the great toe of each foot with the first two fingers and thumbs of your hands to draw your head closer to the mat. If you are able, draw the crown of the head to the floor.
5. If it is too intense, shorten the distance between the feet.
6. Hold for a few breaths, then return to Step 2 and repeat 2–3 times.

TIPS: Keep the muscles of the legs engaged. Press through the outer edges of your feet, almost lifting the inner arch. As you

STANDING SPREAD-LEG   STANDING SPREAD-LEG 2

energetically press down through the outer edges of the feet, energetically draw the inner arch and thigh up in toward the pelvis. The idea in this pose is to keep lifting the navel and draping the upper body over the strong foundation of the legs. As you lift the navel, you can gain more space in the lower back by energetically drawing the thighs toward one another.

Pyramid Pose

1. Begin in Mountain Pose. Step your right foot out in front about 3 feet, or a comfortable stride. Center yourself over your front and back feet, both heels on the floor. Keep both sets of toes facing forward, and keep your hips squared forward.
2. Keeping the legs as straight as possible without locking the knee joints, hinge forward from the hips, dropping the chest toward the front thigh.
3. Keep moving the hips back and the head forward, melting the heart and crown toward the mat.
4. Place your hands where comfortable. They can be on the floor alongside your front foot, or you can interlace your fingers behind you and allow the hands to wrap up and over the crown.
5. Hold for 2–3 breaths. Slowly roll up, drop your hands down to your sides, and step your right foot back into Mountain Pose.
6. Repeat on other side.

TIPS: Root down through the front heel as you draw the front hip back and away from that heel, creating a sensation of traction on that front leg.

PYRAMID   PYRAMID 2

CHAPTER 12

Balancing Postures

Here's what I want you to do: Find a quiet, secluded place so you won't be
tempted to role-play before God. Just be there as simply and honestly as
you can manage. The focus will shift from you to God,
and you will begin to sense his grace.
Matthew 6:6 (The Message)

*B*alancing poses require stamina, focus, and strength. They also develop poise, agility, coordination, and concentration. They require you to draw into your core muscles and awaken overall awareness. They are strengthening poses in which muscle tone is created and precise alignment is essential. Regular practice of balancing postures helps to develop increased control over your physical body.

Balance is essential in your faith walk as well. You have to be willing to give and just as willing to receive. God calls us to be bold in our walks but reminds us that we are strengthened most when we surrender. Manifesting that principle in our bodies through these physical postures helps us to manifest it in our spiritual and emotional bodies as well. Practice coming back to your reliance on Christ as the very center of your being. As the poses become more familiar, you will experience more surrender, just as the more you become familiar with God the more you will be willing to let go and let Him lead you to His place of fullness.

Tree Pose

1. Start in Mountain Pose. Inhale.
2. As you exhale, transfer the weight of your body to your right foot. Place the sole of your left foot on the inside of your right leg just above the ankle, toes pointing to the floor.
3. Slowly draw your left foot upward until it is resting as high on your right leg as is comfortable.
4. Inhaling, draw your hands to heart center in prayer position with thumbs touching your breastbone and fingers toward the ceiling. Keep lengthening the spine.
5. Balance for 6–8 breaths, then repeat on the other side.

TIPS: Be sure the left foot is not pressing into the ankle or knee joints. Soften your tail slightly and drop the shoulders away from the ears, elevating the crown. Bring the left knee back so it is in line with your left hip, keeping the inner thigh and hip open. Stay here if you like or take the hands up overhead bringing your palms together. Maintain the length in your spine and draw the navel in and up for stability.

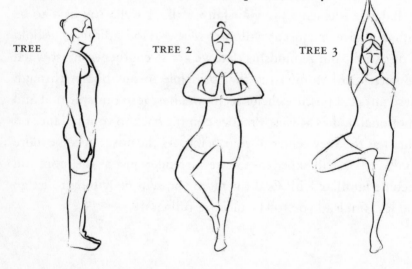

TREE   TREE 2   TREE 3

Boat Pose

1. Begin in a seated position, legs straight out in front of you.
2. Draw your knees into your chest, bringing the feet up off of the floor. Draw your inner thighs together.
3. LEVEL 1: Balance on your sitting bones by pulling the knees in toward the chest while you press the chest into the thighs with the same amount of exertion.

    LEVEL 2: Bring your palms to the back of the thighs and lift the heels so that they are level with the knees. Keep the feet flexed and the legs engaged.

    LEVEL 3: Extend your legs straight out so that your body is now in a V position. Hold for 6–8 breaths if you can. Repeat once or twice if you like.

TIPS: Take this pose to whichever level you are able. Draw the navel in and keep the crown upward lifting. You can keep your arms on your legs, or extend them outward in front or to the side. Keep moving the heart forward and drawing the shoulders back to elevate the heart.

BOAT   BOAT 2   BOAT 3

Half-Moon Pose

1. Begin in Downward Facing Dog.
2. Step your right foot forward between the hands and lift the left leg so you will be balancing on the right foot and leg. Be sure that the left heel is in line with the left hip.
3. Move your right fingertips to about 2 o'clock from your right pinky toe. Inhale and float the left arm up toward the sky, keeping the abdominals engaged.
4. Stack the left hip and lung onto the right hip and lung, imagining the hips, shoulders, and head are against a wall.
5. Keep both legs and arms straight. Open the toes and press all four corners of the right foot into the floor. Either look down to the floor, look straight ahead, or look up toward the sky.
6. Continue to open the left hip by pointing the left great toe and left fingertips toward the sky.
7. Come down into a Standing Forward Fold (see page 162) for rest, then repeat on the other side.

TIPS: Keep the abdominals and pelvic floor muscles contracted. Keep the right leg engaged by lifting the kneecap, flexing the foot, and lifting the inner right thigh. Maintain the length and integrity of your spine by moving the crown forward. Find a point to focus

HALF-MOON   HALF-MOON 2

on. This will help to establish you in the pose. You may use a wall to first experience this pose. The wall will help to establish and strengthen you in the Half-Moon posture.

Revolved Half-Moon Pose

1. Begin in Downward Facing Dog.
2. Step your right foot forward between the hands, squaring the hips over the front leg. Lift the left leg so you will be balancing on the right foot and leg. Be sure that the left heel is in line with the left hip.
3. Set your left fingertips to about 10 o'clock from your right great toe, extending your right arm outward and then upward toward the sky.
4. Open your chest and look up toward your top hand.
5. The hips should be squared to the mat by lifting the left inner thigh toward the ceiling and rotating the left pinky toe toward the mat.
6. Rotate the torso by pressing the left lung forward and drawing the right shoulder and lung back.
7. Come down to Standing Forward Fold (see page 162) for rest and repeat on the other side.

TIPS: Keep the spine straight by moving the crown forward. Really press down through the right hand moving the right lung forward. At the same time, move the left lung back—stacking it onto the right. Keep the length in the left side as you draw the left hip bone back into its socket. Engage every muscle in your body. Be attentive to the sensation of strength.

REVOLVED HALF-MOON   REVOLVED HALF-MOON 2

Warrior 3 Pose

1. Begin in Mountain Pose. Exhale and bend forward from the hip joint, not from the waist. Bring your palms or fingertips to the floor slightly in front of your feet. Inhale.
2. Lift your left leg so that the heel is in line with the hip. Keeping the left foot flexed, press down through the four corners of the right foot.
3. Stretch your arms out like wings to the side and lift the torso until it is parallel to the floor. Keep the left leg engaged with the heel pressing back while extending the crown forward. Lengthen the spine as much as possible while maintaining your balance.
4. If you need to drop the back leg toward the mat, do so. Even having the back leg lifted inches off the mat is beneficial.
5. LEVEL 1: Keep your arms extended out like wings.
   LEVEL 2: Bring your arms out in front of you, parallel to each other, palms facing together. Spread the fingers wide and draw the biceps back by (or even behind) the ears.

6. Hold for 3–5 breaths and come down.

7. Repeat on the other side.

TIPS: The hips should be squared to the mat by lifting the right inner thigh toward the ceiling and rotating the right pinky toe toward the mat. Your crown should be in line with your tail. Engage your core by lifting the navel in and up.

WARRIOR 3–1   WARRIOR 3–2

WARRIOR 3–3

Dancer Pose

1. Start in Mountain Pose.
2. Spread the toes on the right side, rooting in with the 4 corners of the right foot. Transfer your body weight to your right foot and bend your left knee, bringing the heel up backward while you reach for it with your left hand. Place your left foot in the palm of your left hand. Take a moment to balance, then draw the left kneecap in toward the right.
3. Slowly take your right arm up forward, bringing your right bicep next to your right ear. Take a couple of breaths and balance.
4. Working slowly here, begin to press your left foot back behind you, at the same time begin bowing your chest forward. Your body works like a lever here, so press back only as much as you bow forward and vice versa.
5. LEVEL 1: Keep expanding through the heart and chest while you draw the left kneecap in line with the tailbone. Do not splay the knee outward. Stay here for 3–4 breaths and maintain your balance.
   LEVEL 2: Flex your left foot and take the grasp to the left ankle. Press back through the left shin. As you open through the hip, press the right arm forward toward the front of the room and lift it higher. Hold for 3–4 breaths.
   LEVEL 3: Bring your right arm back to the left foot as well, moving the heart forward while opening the chest. Hold for 3–4 breaths.
6. Release and repeat on other side.

TIPS: In Level 1, be sure that your left palm is facing outward and that your left foot is simply sitting on your left palm. If you hold your left foot with the left palm facing in, it closes the hip and shoulder, limiting expansion.

DANCER   DANCER 2   DANCER 3

Extended Leg Pose

1. Start in Mountain Pose.
2. Spread the toes on the right side, rooting in with the 4 corners of the right foot. Transfer your body weight to the right foot and draw the left knee in and up toward the chest. Balance on the right leg, ensuring the spine is long by drawing the navel in and up while you slide the tailbone slightly down.
3. LEVEL 1: Stay here for 4–6 breaths.
   LEVEL 2: Hook your left great toe with the first two fingers and thumb of your left hand. Be sure your left arm is on the inside of the left leg. Begin to straighten your left leg to whatever degree of ability you have in this particular

moment. Keep the left heel pressing forward as the left toes come back toward the nose. Try to lengthen the spine as much as possible by deliberately taking the rounding out of the upper back.

LEVEL 3: Your left leg and spine will be completely straight (without locking the knee). Your shoulders will be stacked over your hips. You can begin to open the hip and foot out to the left if you like.

4. Gently release back to Mountain, pause, and repeat on the other side.

TIPS: Right leg is strong and muscularly engaged without locking the knee joint. Be sure that your left hip bone does not sneak upward. Bring it back into the hip socket. Your left toes should be in line with your left shoulder.

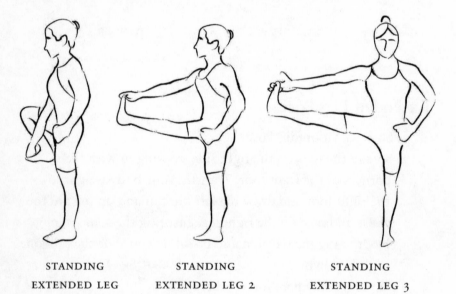

STANDING
EXTENDED LEG

STANDING
EXTENDED LEG 2

STANDING
EXTENDED LEG 3

CHAPTER 13

Arm-Balancing Postures

May he keep us centered and devoted to him,
following the life path he has cleared.
1 Kings 8:58 (The Message)

*A*rm-balancing postures are great for building core strength, confidence, and courage. Like standing postures, they also increase mental awareness. Like balancing postures, they require coordination and concentration. These poses build up the entire body, especially the hands, wrists, arms, shoulders, and core. Success in balancing poses does not come from doing them perfectly but in attempting them with proper awareness of alignment and engagement. When you purposely focus on doing so you will experience both muscular and energetic changes in your body. You will develop in the pose while reaping every benefit along the way.

Arm balances can be a little scary. Try to remember that the floor is not too far away from you. If—I mean, *when*—you fall, you don't have far to go. Liken your fear to the fear of being apart from God. It is terrifying! But the good news is that He is always right there. He's never too far away and always ready to catch us. Our God breaks our fall with grace, tenderness, and mercy. Sometimes I think God just wants us to go for it! He is right there. "If God is for us, who can be against us?" (Rom. 8:31). Take wings here, let yourself soar. God calls us to be bold and promises us He will never leave or forsake us (Deut. 31:6).

Plank Pose

1. Begin in Table Pose (on all fours).
2. Be sure that your wrists are directly under your shoulders and your knees directly under your hips. Energetically melt your heart toward your thumbs so that there is no rounding through the upper back. Soften your tailbone toward the floor slightly and draw your navel in and up toward the small of your back.
3. Turn your toes under so that the pads of your toes are on the floor. Pressing the heels back, roll the weight into the balls of the feet, lift your knees off the floor, and come to a high push-up position.
4. Come out of the pose by pressing back to Tabletop or Child's Pose.

TIPS: Be sure that you are on the balls of both feet, pressing the heels toward the wall behind you. As you press the heels back, draw the inner thighs toward one another and lift them upward toward the ceiling. Keep the legs engaged and the heart soft. Drop to the knees if you get tired, but be sure to keep the spine long.

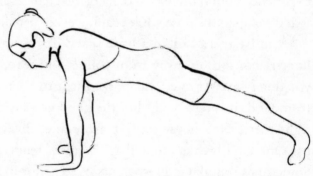

PLANK

Side Arm Balance Pose

1. Begin in Plank Pose.
2. Keeping your right hand on the mat, bring it directly under your nose.
3. Shift your weight to the outer edge of your right foot and lift your left foot off the mat, stacking the left foot onto the right, toes to heel, if your body permits.
4. Take your left hand up toward the heavens.
5. As you move the right side of the body slightly forward, draw the left side of the body slightly back—stacking the hips and the shoulders
6. LEVEL 1: Hold in this position for 3–4 breaths.
   LEVEL 2: Take the left bicep by the left ear and reach toward the front of the room. Optional—lift the left foot off of the right.
   LEVEL 3: Hook the great toe of the left foot with the first two fingers and thumb of the left hand and extend the left leg upward, keeping hold of the great toe.
7. Release, and repeat on the other side.

TIPS: You can always drop the right knee to the mat for a gentler version. As you root down through your right hand from the center of the chest, reach upward with the left hand from the center of the chest. Energetically exert the same amount of emphasis with both arms. Open the chest and engage the core by drawing the navel in and up. Legs are strong. Lift the left hip upward. Lengthen the leg as far upward as possible without locking the knee joint.

SIDE ARM BALANCE   SIDE ARM BALANCE 2

Crow Pose

1. Start in Mountain Pose, taking your feet a little wider than hip-width apart.
2. Lift all 10 toes and press in through the outer edges of both feet to get rooted. Take a deep bend in both knees coming into a squat position. Drop your tail toward the floor and lift your navel in and up.
3. If you can, place your heels to the mat. If not, stay on the balls of the feet, not gripping with the toes. Bring your hands to your heart center and begin to press the heart toward the hands.
4. Press your palms into one another, moving triceps firmly into the inner thighs. Energetically hug the inner thighs against your triceps.
5. Keeping that engagement between the thighs and the triceps, place your hands on the mat about 2 inches in front of the toes.
6. Lift the tail up and roll the weight into the hands. Be sure

the thighs are still squeezing the upper arms. Take your gaze about 6 inches in front of you on the mat.

7. Roll onto your tiptoes, moving the weight into the hands.

8. LEVEL 1: If this is as far as you can go, rest here for 4–6 breaths.

   LEVEL 2: If you can, start by lifting one set of toes off the mat and then add the other. (It may take you days, weeks, or even months to get both sets of toes off the mat.)

9. Once both feet are off the floor, try to touch the great toes together.

10. As you bring the great toes together, imagine there is a block between your inner thighs; draw the energy of your thighs in toward one another. You will feel your tail lift. Draw your navel in and upward to take any sway out of your lower back.

11. Hold your final pose for 4–6 breaths, then gently lower your feet and return to Mountain.

TIPS: Make sure the gaze is moving forward; your weight will follow your gaze.

CROW   CROW 2

Yoga Push-Up

(High to Low Push-Up Position)

1. Begin in Plank Pose.
2. Keeping the entire body engaged, roll the body forward to the tiptoes.
3. Be sure that the inner eyes (creases) of the elbows are facing forward. Hinge at the elbows and begin to bring your body down toward the mat.
4. Pause for a breath in the low position.
5. Really press through the heels of the hands and come back up.
6. Repeat 2–3 times if you can.

TIPS: Keep your eyes focused out in front of you. Keep the body taut as you lower down. Really lift up your navel to remove the sway in the lower back. Keep the elbows moving back *alongside* the body. When you are at the bottom of your push-up, your thumbs should be in line with the center of the chest. For a gentler version, drop the knees to the mat on the way up and/or the way down.

YOGA PUSH-UP 2

YOGA PUSH-UP

YOGA PUSH-UP 3

CHAPTER 14

Inverted Postures

I'll refresh tired bodies; I'll restore tired souls.
Jeremiah 31:25 (The Message)

nverted poses reverse the effects of gravity, stimulating the entire system. They replenish the brain and rejuvenate the organs and glandular system by reversing the normal flow of blood and lymph. After an inversion, the normal circulatory patterns are restored with new vitality. Inversions also strengthen the upper body and nervous system as well as improve digestion and elimination. They require focus and concentration and create clarity of perception and an overall sensation of calm. They are usually avoided during pregnancy and menstruation.

Inversions are the ultimate in Holy Yoga poses. They refresh, rejuvenate, and make our bodies come alive with increased energy and vitality. Isn't that a great metaphor of our God? He does refresh, rejuvenate, and encourage us to "come alive" in Him. Sometimes God turns us upside down, getting us out of our comfort zones to remind us of our great need for His abundance.

It is not every day that I long to be throwing my feet up over my head or propping myself up against a wall gazing up at my toes that are in desperate need of a good pedicure—just as it is not every day that I long to be turned upside down and inside out by

God. I know, however, that God *will* replenish me. He will wash me in a sea of grace. He will give me a showering of joy and peace known only through Him. Even if He has to flip me around a bit . . . turning everything I think I know upside down. I can rest assured that everything will come out right side up.

Fun? Not always. Comfortable? Not even close. Worth it? Every single moment. Enjoy the time you have with God in these inverted poses. Let His magnificence be magnified . . . even if you are upside down.

Shoulder Stand Pose

1. Start by lying flat on the floor, knees bent with the soles of the feet to the mat.
2. Place your hands under your lower back for support, dropping your elbows into the mat.
3. LEVEL 1: Lift your feet up off of the floor, drawing the knees toward your face, and lift your legs upward toward the ceiling. Push yourself up so that your hips are off the mat, still supporting your lower back with your hands, legs straight and toes pointed at the sky. Hold in this position for 3–4 breaths.
   LEVEL 2: If you like, you can begin to move the hands up toward the mid-back to get the hips and legs more vertical.
   LEVEL 3: Take your hands away from the back, interlacing the fingers down to the knuckles. Press the entire length of the arms firmly into the mat so that they become a strong base for the vertical position of your spine.
4. Gently release and return your legs to the mat.

TIPS: Engage the legs and core while you fan the toes wide. Most importantly, press the back of the skull into the mat, lifting the chin up off of the chest. Be sure that the neck is not pressing flat into the mat but that the natural curve in the neck is maintained. *Do not* compromise your neck by pressing it flat into the mat.

SHOULDER STAND   SHOULDER STAND 2   SHOULDER STAND 3

Plow Pose

1. Start by lying flat on the floor, knees bent with the soles of the feet to the mat.
2. Place your hands under your lower back for support, dropping your elbows into the mat.
3. When you feel completely supported, take your feet up off of the floor, lifting the legs upward toward the ceiling.
4. Hinging from the hips, drop the legs up and over the head, so that the toes are behind the head.
5. Keep the hands on the lower back if you would like, or begin to move the hands up toward the mid-back for more support.
6. If your toes touch the floor behind you, try to roll the balls of the feet to the floor, pressing the heels back behind you.
7. Rest here for 3–4 breaths, then gently release and return your legs to the mat.

TIPS: Engage the legs and core while you fan the toes wide. Most importantly, press the back of the skull into the mat, lifting the chin up off of the chest. Be sure that the neck is not pressing flat into the mat, but that the natural curve in the neck is maintained. *Do not* compromise your neck by pressing it flat into the mat. Engage the legs by squeezing the muscles to the bones. Your inner thighs will come inward and lift upward with engagement, allowing for the sitting bones to broaden.

PLOW   PLOW 2   PLOW 3

Legs-Up-the-Wall Pose

1. Start by sitting on the floor sideways next to a wall that is suitable for working against. Your right hip should be against the wall.
2. Place the soles of the feet on the floor so that the knees are bent, keeping the spine vertical.
3. Exhaling, lie back onto the floor perpendicular to the wall, swinging your outstretched legs up onto the wall. Your legs will be completely supported by the wall.
4. Place your hands or a folded blanket underneath your lower back if it would be more comfortable.
5. Hold for 2–3 minutes while using any of the yoga breathing techniques.

TIPS: This pose is an inversion you can do even if you are menstruating since you are not inverting the hips. Keep the chin up off of the chest by pressing the back side of the skull into the mat—it is *essential* to maintain the natural curve in your neck.

LEGS UP WALL

Headstand Pose

Note: If you are a beginner, you may move your mat near a wall or a corner. You can use the wall to support your legs as you are learning. It is also advisable to have a friend help you as you get used to inverting your entire body.

1. Begin in Tabletop Pose. Drop your forearms to the floor and interlace your fingers. Open your wrists outward, forming a hollow in your hands.
2. Press down with the forearms, becoming aware of the foundation you are setting.
3. Place the crown of your head in the hollow of your hands so that the interlaced fingers are just behind the crown, cradling your skull.
4. Move the weight of your body forward onto the crown, moving the hips forward and pressing the forearms down.
5. If you feel comfortable, tuck your toes (leaving them on the floor) and begin to lift your hips up, just like Downward

Facing Dog but with the forearms and crown in the mat.

6. Keep a bend in the knees if necessary and begin to walk the feet closer toward the head.

7. You want to bring your hips forward enough that they stack onto the shoulders, keeping your feet on the floor as you do so.

8. LEVEL 1: Stay here if you are newer. As you get more comfortable, you can move closer to a full inversion by lifting one foot off of the floor. As you increase your balance and spatial awareness, you will be able to move into full headstand.

   LEVEL 2: If you are ready for a full headstand, root into the mat with your forearms *before* you attempt to fully invert. Your neck *cannot* withstand the entire weight of your body. You *must* support the weight with your forearms. Slowly lift your legs up straight.

9. Stay here for 8–10 breaths before coming down in to a Child's Pose for at least 4–5 breaths. You need to recover from the bloodbath you just gave your brain. If you whip your head upright immediately after a headstand, you run a serious risk of passing out.

TIPS: It is most important to keep your core engaged. Feel as though your navel is pulling inward to help reduce any sway in the lower back. Once you are in your headstand, draw your shoulders away from your ears. This will ensure that your arms are rooted and that you are using your arms to bear the weight of your body. Keep your entire body energetically engaged, reaching upward with your feet and inward with your navel.

HEADSTAND

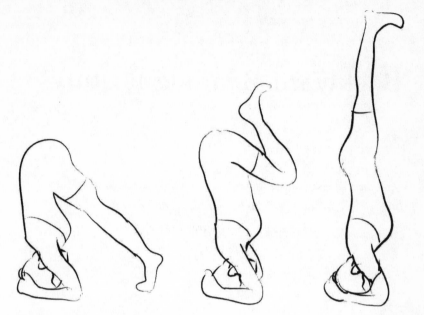

HEADSTAND 2   HEADSTAND 3   HEADSTAND 4

CHAPTER 15

Backward-Bending Postures

And the God of all grace, who called you to his eternal glory in Christ,
after you have suffered a little while, will himself restore you
and make you strong, firm and steadfast.

1 Peter 5:10

*B*ack bends are rejuvenating and awakening. They are effective at opening the upper back, chest, neck, shoulders, and front groin as well as increasing spinal flexibility. They keep the spine supple while developing strength in the back, legs, and shoulders. Back bends should not be practiced close to the time of sleep as they create heat and can cause mild insomnia. Back bends come from leg strength, so be sure that your legs are engaged as a foundation to any back bend. They should be followed by a series of cooling poses such as forward bends to allow the spine to realign.

Back bends release trapped emotional energy better than any other class of poses. They get into the back sides of our bodies where we most readily store stuff from our past experiences. Since we live in a fallen world, we have undoubtedly been lied to, cheated on, stolen from, or slandered somewhere along the way. As energetic creations, we accumulate energy associated with our experiences. Good experiences leave good energetic impressions that manifest in our physical bodies, and bad experiences leave bad ones.

We carry those negative imprints around with us, continually making them our personal truth. Our Father calls us to cast our burdens upon Him (1 Pet. 5:7). He gives us a way of authentically lightening our load so that we can get better at *knowing* Him. Release those burdens to Him. Let His loving grace include the energetic and physical freedom you have been searching for.

Cat/Cow Pose

1. Begin in Tabletop Pose.
2. Be sure that the palms are spread flat and that all 10 fingertips are pressing into the mat—not gripping, but aware of the connection.
3. Bring the shoulders directly over the wrists and the hips directly over the knees.

CAT/COW

4. Cow Pose: Lift your crown and tail simultaneously upward, allowing your belly to soften toward the floor.
5. Cat Pose: Pressing firmly in with the palms, draw your navel in and up and tuck your tail and crown toward the floor at the same time. Really arch the upper back around the back side of the heart.

CAT/COW 2

6. Flow this a few times, inhaling as you come into Cow and exhaling into Cat, replenishing the spine.

CAT/COW 3

TIPS: Let the movement in the spine start from the tailbone, so that the neck is the last to move. In Cow, curl your toes under so that the pads of your toes are on the floor. In Cat, release the tops of the feet to the floor.

Sphinx Pose

1. Lie on your belly, legs at hip width, tops of the feet on the floor. Relax your forehead on the mat.
2. Start by bringing the chin to the mat. Place your forearms, palms down, on the mat so that the tops of the fingers are in line with the tops of the shoulders.
3. Inhaling, press your forearms into the floor and begin to lift your chest and head. Look straight ahead. Pelvis stays on the mat.
4. Bring your elbows directly under the shoulders and press down through the forearms and heels of the hands. Lengthen your spine as much as possible, then draw your shoulders and forearms back while lifting the crown upward.
5. Stay in the pose 6–8 breaths.
6. Relax out of the pose by releasing the upper body back to the mat and bring your cheek to the floor.

TIPS: Maintain the length in the spine by dropping the shoulders away from the ears and extending the crown upward. Keep the lower body soft until you are fully in the pose. You want to *lengthen* your spine, so if you are clenching your buttocks and legs, it will be impossible to get the length you desire. As you press through the forearms and heels of the hands, draw your shoulder blades back behind your heart, essentially pressing your heart forward through the shoulders. Feel your hands energetically pull the mat back in a traction type of action.

SPHINX

SPHINX 2

SPHINX 3

Cobra Pose

1. Lie on your belly, legs at hip-width, tops of the feet on the floor. Relax your forehead on the mat.
2. Start by bringing the chin to the mat. Place your forearms, palms down, on the mat so that the fingertips are in line with the tops of the shoulders.
3. Inhaling, press your forearms into the floor and begin to lift your chest and head. Look straight ahead. Pelvis stays on the mat.
4. Spread all 10 fingertips wide and press down through the heels of the hands, drawing the shoulder blades back and down away from the ears. Extend the crown upward toward the heavens, keeping the buttocks soft until you lengthen as much as possible.
5. Begin to press the palms down, lifting the elbows off of the mat. Raise your chest and head as high as you feel comfortable, keeping your elbows bent.
6. Stay here for a few breaths and then come out of the pose by releasing the body down to the mat, bringing the opposite cheek to the mat.

TIPS: Bring the elbows in alongside the body, being sure that the elbows point back. Once the spine is fully lengthened and the chest is opened, engage the lower body by pressing the thighs down into the mat. To make this pose easier, move your hands forward. To make it more challenging, move your hands farther back.

COBRA

COBRA 2

COBRA 3

Locust Pose

1. Lie on your belly with one cheek on the floor. Start by bringing the chin to the floor.

2. Keeping your chin there, lengthen your arms alongside the body so that the palms are facing down and the fingertips are reaching for the wall behind you.

3. Begin to lift your head and chest up off the floor. The crown of the head will be lengthening forward directly in front of you, so the gaze will be directly under your nose.

4. LEVEL 1: Stay here if it is comfortable.

   LEVEL 2: Lift the right leg up and back. Pointing the toes, reach with them for the wall behind you.

LEVEL 3: Lift both legs, pointing the toes toward the wall in back.

5. Hold the pose for a few breaths and release, bringing the opposite cheek to the mat for rest.

TIPS: If you desire, you can bring the biceps by the ears, fanning your fingers wide as you reach forward with your fingertips. Feel free to take legs and arms up at the same time, or opposite arm and leg. Any variation is fine, just stay with your breath and stay conscious of the sensation. Keep the legs engaged by lifting the inner thighs inward and upward.

LOCUST   LOCUST 2

Upward Facing Dog Pose

1. Lie on your belly with one cheek on the floor. Start by bringing the chin to the floor. Keeping your chin there, bring your fingertips in line with the tops of the shoulders.

2. Spread all 10 fingertips wide and press down through the heels of the hands, drawing the shoulder blades back and down away from the ears. Extend the crown upward toward the heavens, keeping the buttocks soft until you lengthen as much as possible.

3. Begin to press the palms down, lifting the upper body. You will straighten your arms as much as possible here.

4. You can leave your thighs resting on the mat, or you can engage the thighs by drawing the inner thighs toward one

another and then upward. Your thighs will lift off the floor as you press firmly into the mat with the tops of your feet.

5. Stay here for a few breaths and then release, bringing the opposite cheek to the floor.

TIPS: Your crown will move upward, away from the ears as you drop the shoulder blades down the back side of the body. Your chest will broaden and your heart will move forward, almost like a pendulum, through the shoulders. Depending on your ability, you may straighten your arms to enhance the back bend. Be sure the heels of your hands are pressing down firmly, your elbow joints stay soft, and that you do not clench your buttocks.

UPWARD FACING DOG

UPWARD FACING DOG 2

UPWARD FACING DOG 3

UPWARD FACING DOG 4

Camel Pose

1. Start in a kneeling position, shoulders stacked directly over the hips, shins, and tops of the feet on the floor. From your knees to your crown should be a straight line upward.

2. Bring your hands to your lower back for support. The

fingertips can be facing downward or upward depending on the flexibility of your wrists.

3. Engage the legs by pressing the tops of the feet into the mat and squeezing the inner thighs in toward one another as if there were an imaginary block between them (they will not be touching). As you do, draw the tailbone slightly down and forward to protect the lower back.

4. Use your hands to press your hips forward over the knees, drawing your elbows toward one another back behind you.

5. LEVEL 1: Stay here with your hands on your lower back for a few breaths.

   LEVEL 2: Tuck your toes so that the balls of the feet are touching the floor behind you and bring one or both hands to your heels.

   LEVEL 3: Keep your hands on your heels and drop the tops of the feet back to the mat. Your gaze will be up and backward, on the ceiling or on the wall behind you.

6. Come out of the pose and rest in Tabletop position. Flow a couple of Cat/Cow poses to replenish and realign the spine.

TIPS: It's important that the hips are pressing forward over the knees. If your hips fall behind your knees, come out of the pose a bit and work there so as not to compromise your lower back. By bringing your hands back, the shoulder blades come behind the heart, bolstering it upward.

CAMEL   CAMEL 2   CAMEL 3

Bridge Pose

1. Begin by lying on your back. Bend the knees so that the soles of the feet are flat on the floor.

2. Bring the heels about 3–5 inches from the tail and spread the toes nice and wide. Place your hands alongside your body on the mat with the palms facing down.

3. LEVEL 1: As you press in through the soles of the feet, begin to lift the hips up toward the ceiling. Bring the hips up only as much as is comfortable, remembering that back bends are designed to heal the spine, not hurt it.

BRIDGE

BRIDGE 2

LEVEL 2: You can interlace your fingers down to the knuckles underneath you, really drawing the shoulder blades onto your back body. Feel your heart lift upward as your hips elevate just a bit more.

BRIDGE 3

4. Stay in your Bridge for 3–4 breaths and then gently release, rolling down a vertebrae at a time.

SUPPORTED BRIDGE

5. Either draw your knees into your chest or bring the soles of the feet together, allowing the knees to fall apart and outward from one another to reset the spine.

TIPS: Really press in with the hands and the soles of the feet, as they are your foundation. As if there were a block between your thighs, energetically draw them toward one another. Feel your kneecaps draw forward, lengthening the tops of your thighs. Be sure that the natural curve in your neck is maintained by pressing the back of the skull into the mat and drawing the chin up and off of the chest. Really use your arms as a foundation here by pressing them both firmly into the mat.

Bow Pose

1. Lie on your belly with one cheek on the floor. Start by bringing the chin to the floor. Keeping your chin there, bend the knees and flex the feet so that the soles of the feet are facing upward.
2. Reach back with your hands for either the ankles or the top of the feet.
3. Strongly lift your heels away from your buttocks and lift your thighs away from the floor. Pull your chest and head off the floor, opening the chest.
4. Stay here for a few breaths
5. Gently release and lie back down, bringing the opposite cheek to the mat.

TIPS: Really focus on opening the chest by softening the shoulders away from the ears. Your gaze can be forward or downward, depending on how your neck feels. If your hands are on your ankles, really flex the feet and press your shins back. Be sure that your knees are not splaying outward, but that your inner thighs are drawing inward toward one another. The knees should be in line with the hips.

BOW 1

BOW 2   BOW 3

Wheel Pose

1. Begin by lying on your back. Bend the knees so that the soles of the feet are flat on the floor. Bring the heels about 3–5 inches from the tail and spread the toes nice and wide.

2. Bring your hands up by your shoulders, placing the palms flat to the mat with the fingertips tucked behind the shoulders.

3. Lift your hips, attempting to get them in line with your knees or as close as possible.

4. Maintain the natural curve in your neck by pressing the back of the skull firmly into the mat and drawing your chin up and off of your chest.

5. LEVEL 1: Pressing in through the palms, bring the top of the head to the mat. Draw the elbows toward one another and bring the shoulder blades onto the back body.
LEVEL 2: If you want more, press through the heels of the hands and lift the crown up off of the floor.
LEVEL 3: Begin to straighten the legs by pressing through the heels while you move your heart toward the wall behind you. Keep moving the shoulders away from the ears, allowing the natural weight of the crown to lengthen the neck.

6. Breathe there for as long as you can without straining.
7. To come down, bend the elbows and place the crown back onto the floor.
8. Release the spine back to the mat a vertebrae at a time.
9. Draw the knees into the chest and gently rock back and forth, massaging the back.
10. Repeat if desired.

TIPS: Back bends are leg-strength poses. Press through the heels and engage the legs so that the lower back is supported. As though there were a block between your thighs, energetically draw your inner thighs in to support the lower back.

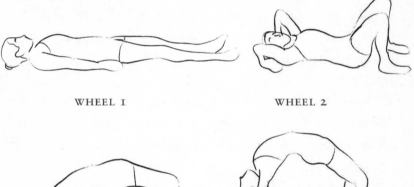

WHEEL 1   WHEEL 2

WHEEL 3   WHEEL 4

Fish Pose

1. Start by lying on your back.
2. Slide your hands beneath your lower back, directly under the sacrum (tailbone). Touch your first fingers together and thumbs together, making a diamond shape.
3. Bending your elbows, push your chest upward on the forearms and elbows.
4. Make sure that the elbows are pointing straight back behind you. Draw your shoulder blades way back, as if you were holding a penny between them, and lift your heart upward.
5. Stay here if you like, or allow your head to tilt back, really exposing the throat and resting the crown on the mat.
6. Stay here for 3–4 breaths. Release and repeat multiple times if desired.

TIPS: Draw your shoulders away from the ears hard by pressing down through your forearms. Be sure that your lower body is active and the legs are engaged to support the lower back.

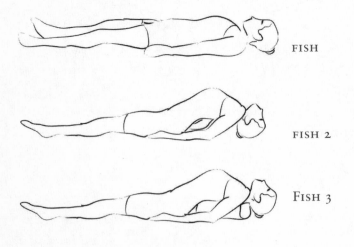

FISH

FISH 2

FISH 3

CHAPTER 16

Twisting Postures

Wash away all my iniquity and cleanse me from my sin.
Psalm 51:2

*T*wists are a unique class of postures because they are cooling and soothing after back bends, yet stimulating after forward bends. They are sometimes referred to as "smart poses" because they cleanse the body, giving it what it needs to return to balance. Twists massage and tone the entire abdominal cavity and detoxify the glands and organs. In addition, they replenish the circulation to the spinal muscles and disks, creating hydration and mobility. They squeeze the abdominal organs as the trunk rotates, allowing fresh blood to surge into organs. Note: If you are pregnant or have chronic back ailments, be sure to use gentle variations of the twists.

The most important thing to remember about twists is to maintain the integrity of the spine by *lengthening before twisting*. If you ever feel as though your length is compromised, come out of the twist a bit and breathe there. As you create space and healing in the pose with the breath (fresh oxygen and blood), you will be able to move deeper into the pose without injuries. It may not be today or even tomorrow, but there is no rush. You have nothing but time to enjoy, to embrace, and to be fully immersed in the gift of life, of breath, and of grace.

Gentle Seated Twist

1. Start sitting with your legs outstretched in front of you. Draw the sole of the right foot to the inner thigh of the left leg, being sure that the right heel is as close to the groin as possible.
2. Bring the left foot in toward the right. The left sole can rest on the right shin.
3. Move the excess flesh away from the sitting bones, so that your tail feels connected to the mat.
4. Place your right hand on the left knee and begin to twist your torso to the left.
5. You can leave both hands there or begin to bring your left hand behind you for more twist.
6. If you use your left hand, really press it down into the mat to maintain the length in the spine, then twist by moving your right lung forward as you move your left lung back.
7. Stay there for a few breaths and then release.
8. Repeat on the other side

TIPS: Be sure that your spine is straight, extending the crown upward, dropping the shoulders away from the ears, and drawing the shoulder blades back behind the heart.

SEATED GENTLE TWIST

SEATED GENTLE TWIST 2

Seated Spinal Twist 1

1. Start sitting with your legs outstretched in front of you. Bend the right knee and set the right sole of the foot on the floor alongside the left inner thigh.
2. Reach the right arm forward as far as you can, with the arm to the inside of the right bent leg.
3. Reach the right arm around the bent right knee.
4. Be sure to hug the inner right thigh in toward the midline and maintain that energetically throughout the pose, regardless of level.
5. LEVEL 1: Stay here if this feels right to you.
   LEVEL 2: Bring your left hand around your back and clasp the left wrist with the right hand. Use a strap here if you need to.
   LEVEL 3: With a straight spine and hands bound, hinge from the hips forward into a Seated Forward Fold (see page 161).
6. Stay in your final pose (wherever you are) for 3–4 breaths, then release. Repeat on the other side.

TIPS: As you draw the left hand back, open the chest and lengthen the spine by extending the crown upward. Be sure to keep the heart open and the left outstretched leg engaged.

SEATED SPINAL TWIST 1   SEATED SPINAL TWIST 1–2

Lying Spinal Twist (with Variation)

1. Start lying flat on your mat with your legs outstretched. Draw both knees into your chest, draping the hands just below your knees so that the tops of the thighs soften into the belly and chest.

2. Open your arms out like wings, pressing the palms into the mat.

3. Bring your knees to a 90-degree angle, so that the knees stack over the hips and the heels are in line with the knees.

4. Draw the inner thighs tightly toward one another and then drop both knees to the right. Hold for 1–2 breaths.

5. LEVEL 1: Bring knees back to center, using your core strength, then drop them to the left and hold for 1–2 breaths.

   LEVEL 2: When dropping the knees to the right and left, keep the knees and thighs elevated off of the mat an inch or two on each side, using your core strength to keep the legs lifted.

6. Draw the knees back into the chest when finished, rocking back and forth on the mat to massage the lower back.

LYING SPINAL TWIST

LYING SPINAL TWIST 2

One-Leg Variation

1. While lying flat on the mat, bring just the right knee in to the chest, keeping the left leg outstretched.
2. Engage the left leg by flexing the toes back toward the nose and anchoring the left inner thigh down toward the mat.
3. Open the arms out like wings and drop the right knee over to the left side of the body. Lengthen from the right hip to the right kneecap.
4. You can rest the left hand on the right knee if you would like, keeping the left lung lifting upward.
5. Hold for 2–3 breaths, then repeat on the other side.

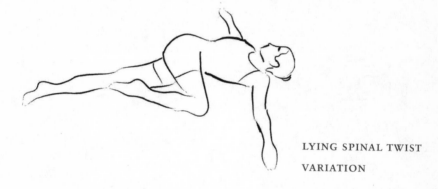

LYING SPINAL TWIST
VARIATION

Revolved Crescent Lunge Pose

1. Begin in Downward Facing Dog.
2. Step the right foot forward and place it on the mat between your hands.
3. Stay on the ball of the left foot. You can drop the knee if necessary.
4. Bring your left hand to the floor inside of the right foot.
5. Take your right hand upward, twisting the torso.
6. Hold for 2–3 breaths and release. Repeat other side.

CRESCENT LUNGE   REVOLVED CRESCENT

REVOLVED CRESCENT 2

CHAPTER 17

Forward-Bending Postures

Be agreeable, be sympathetic, be loving, be compassionate, be humble.
1 Peter 3:8 (The Message)

Forward bends are calming, soothing to the nervous system, and they bring a deeper internal awareness. They open the entire back side of the body, stretching the hamstrings, buttocks, and lower back. They release tension and improve digestion and elimination by massaging the abdominal organs and cleansing the liver and intestines. Seated-forward bends increase circulation to the lower extremities and bathe the brain with fresh blood and oxygen.

The forward-bending postures are my favorite for worship and prayer. In the Bible, it was common for people to bow low or prostrate themselves in worship. Whenever I am folded forward, I imagine I'm bowing before God, praising Him with everything I am.

Pigeon Pose

1. Start in Downward Facing Dog.
2. Bring your right knee forward between the hands and place

it on the floor, simultaneously dropping the left knee to the floor.

3. Draw your right heel in toward the groin as much as possible and turn your left hip downward. The most important thing is to square the hips toward the floor. Once squared, drop the left knee back to the mat.

4. Fold forward over the bent right knee, outstretching the arms in front of you. Melt your chest toward the mat, close your eyes, and rest here for 3–4 breaths.

5. Repeat on the other side for the same length of time

TIPS: To emphasize, tuck your left toes to the mat and lift the left knee. Your inner left thigh will be lifting upward, spinning the left hip bone and pinky toe toward the mat. Use a block or towel under your right hip if it would be more comfortable.

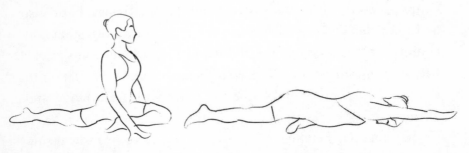

PIGEON   PIGEON 2

Seated Forward Fold Pose

1. Start by sitting on your mat with your legs stretched out in front of you. Rest directly on your sitting bones by using your hands to move the fleshy excess away from your hips and buttocks.

2. Lengthen the spine upward toward the ceiling, drawing

your shoulder blades onto your back body behind the heart.

3. Keeping a straight spine, begin to hinge forward from the hips.

4. Bring your hands alongside your thighs. As you press in with your palms, draw your elbows back alongside the body and move your heart forward toward your shins.

5. Rest for 3–5 breaths, then release.

TIPS: Engage the legs by flexing the feet. Press the heels away from you forward and rotate your inner thighs down into the mat. Without locking the knee joints, your legs should be strong and engaged. A tight lower back comes from tight hips and hamstrings, so be gentle with your expectations. As you hinge, draw your navel inward and upward. Do not compromise the length or integrity of the spine by caving your shoulders forward. It is not about how close the chest gets to the thighs— it is more about length and protecting your lower back and hamstrings.

SEATED FORWARD FOLD

SEATED FORWARD FOLD 2

SEATED FORWARD FOLD 3

Standing Forward Fold Pose

1. Start in Mountain Pose with feet hip width apart.
2. Gently hinge from the hips into a forward fold. Bend the knees as you begin.
3. You will feel a lot of pressure in your head and neck. Gently move your head from left to right and forward to back to release any tension.
4. LEVEL 1: Try to relax here, regulating your breath and bathing your brain with fresh oxygen and blood.
   LEVEL 2: Take your palms to the calves, bending your elbows toward the back of the room.
5. Relax wherever is comfortable for 4–6 breaths.
6. Release the pose by stepping back to a Downward Facing Dog, or unhinge from the hips, coming back up to standing with a straight spine.

TIPS: In Level 1, try not to grip the mat with your toes. Try lifting all 10 of them up off of the mat as you root down through all 4 corners of each foot. Legs are engaged but the knee joints are not locked. Rest your fingertips or hands to the mat or to

STANDING FORWARD FOLD   STANDING FORWARD FOLD 2   STANDING FORWARD FOLD 3

a block. In Level 2, as you bend your elbows, your chest and upper back will broaden, allowing you to draw your heart closer in toward your thighs. Try to spin your inner thighs back toward the wall behind you. In doing so, the sitting bones will rotate outward and the tailbone will have room to extend up and back, creating more space in the lower spine and sacrum.

Head-to-Knee Forward Pose

1. Start by sitting on your mat with your legs stretched out in front of you.
2. Bring the sole of the right foot toward you and place it onto the inner edge of the left thigh, allowing the right knee and thigh to rest on the floor.
3. Find your sitting bones by moving the fleshy excess away from your hips and buttocks. Lengthen the spine upward by extending the spine toward the ceiling and drawing your shoulder blades onto your back body behind the heart.
4. Keeping a straight spine, turn your shoulders to square directly over the left outstretched leg and begin to hinge forward from the hips.
5. Bring your hands alongside your left thigh. As you press in with your palms, draw your elbows back alongside the body and move your heart forward toward your left leg.
6. Rest wherever is comfortable for 2–3 breaths, then release and repeat on other side.

TIPS: Engage the left leg by flexing the foot and rotating the inner thigh down toward the floor—without locking the knee joint. A tight lower back comes from tight hamstrings, so be gentle with your expectations. As you hinge, draw your navel inward and upward allowing your chest to move forward. *Do not* compromise the length or integrity of the spine by caving your shoulders forward. It is not about how close the chest gets to the thighs—it is more important to protect your lower back and hamstrings.

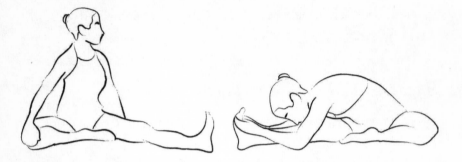

HEAD-TO-KNEE   HEAD-TO-KNEE 2

Revolved Head-to-Knee Pose

1. Start by sitting on your mat with your legs stretched out in front of you. Bring the sole of the right foot toward you and place it onto the inner edge of the left thigh, allowing the right knee and thigh to rest on the floor.

2. Find your sitting bones by moving the fleshy excess away from your hips and buttocks. As you do, lengthen the spine upward by extending the spine toward the ceiling and drawing your shoulder blades onto your back body behind the heart.

3. LEVEL 1: Bring your left elbow to the interior of the left thigh, either onto the floor or onto a block. As you do, take your right arm high toward the ceiling.
   LEVEL 2: Take your right hand toward the left foot, either by bringing the right bicep by the ear or grabbing the left toes with the right hand.

4. Be sure that you do not cave forward with the right lung. Press the left lung forward as you draw the right lung back, essentially stacking the right lung onto the left.

5. Rest here for 2–3 breaths, then come out and repeat on the other side.

TIPS: In Level 1, engage the left leg by flexing the foot and rotating the inner thigh down toward the floor—without locking the knee joint. Keep the right lung back so that you are not caving forward.

REVOLVED HEAD-TO-KNEE 1

REVOLVED HEAD-TO-KNEE 2

REVOLVED HEAD-TO-KNEE 3

REVOLVED HEAD-TO-KNEE 4

Seated Open-Angle Pose

1. Start by sitting on your mat with your legs stretched out in front of you. Open your legs wide in an open V formation.
2. Try to find your sitting bones by moving the fleshy excess away from your hips and buttocks. As you do, lengthen the spine upward by extending the spine toward the ceiling and drawing your shoulder blades onto your back body behind the heart.
3. Keeping a straight spine, begin to hinge from the hips forward.
4. Bring your hands forward onto the floor and begin walking them toward the front of the room. As you press in with your palms, draw your heart forward toward the mat.
5. Hold at your comfortable point for 3–4 breaths. Gently release.

TIPS: Engage the legs by flexing the feet. Press the heels away from you forward, and rotate your inner thighs down into the mat. Without locking the knee joints, legs should be strong and engaged. A tight lower back comes from tight hamstrings,

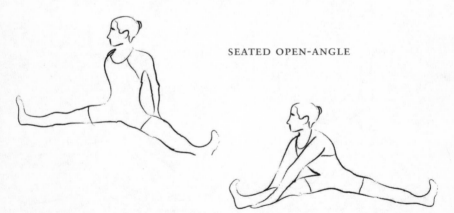

SEATED OPEN-ANGLE

SEATED OPEN-ANGLE 2

SEATED OPEN-ANGLE 3

so be gentle with your expectations. As you hinge, draw your navel inward and upward. Do not compromise the length or integrity of the spine by caving your shoulders forward. It is not about how close the chest gets to the thighs—it is more important to protect your lower back and hamstrings.

Seated Open-Angle Side Pose

1. Start by sitting on your mat with your legs stretched out in front of you. Open your legs wide in an open V formation.
2. Try to find your sitting bones by moving the fleshy excess away from your hips and buttocks. As you do, lengthen the spine upward by extending the spine toward the ceiling and drawing your shoulder blades onto your back body behind the heart.
3. Without locking the knee joints, legs should be strong and engaged. Bring your left elbow to the interior of the left thigh, either onto the floor or onto a block. As you do, take your right arm high toward the ceiling.
4. LEVEL 1: Keep the right lung back so that you are not caving forward with the right lung.
   LEVEL 2: Take your right hand toward the left foot, either by bringing the right bicep by the ear or grabbing the left toes with the right hand.
5. Hold for 1–2 breaths and release. Repeat on the other side.

TIPS: Engage the legs by flexing the feet. Press the heels away from you forward and rotate your inner thighs down into the mat. Be sure that you do not cave forward with the right lung. Press the left lung forward as you draw the right lung back, essentially stacking the right lung onto the left.

SEATED OPEN-ANGLE SIDE

SEATED OPEN-ANGLE SIDE 2

SEATED OPEN-ANGLE SIDE 3

Splits

1. Start by coming into a lunge on the right side, dropping the left knee to the floor.
2. Open up the pelvic floor by moving the left knee back.
3. Flex the right foot so that the heel is rooted into the mat.
4. Breathe into the back side of the knee joint, drawing the right hip bone back into the hip socket.
5. Begin to move the left knee farther back on your mat until you reach your edge.
6. Hold for a breath or two, then come out of the pose and repeat on opposite side.

TIPS: *Do not push it!* Breathe and grow into your pose. You can ease the pose by sitting on a blanket or a block to help support the weight of your body.

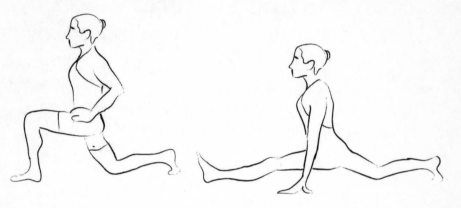

SPLITS

SPLITS 2

SPLITS 3

SUPPORTED SPLITS

CHAPTER 18

Sitting Postures

*I will bring health and healing to it; I will heal my people
and will let them enjoy abundant peace and security.*
Jeremiah 33:6

*S*itting and meditation postures are generally calming and
nurturing, although some produce significant opening of
the hip and require greater effort. They promote vitality when
practiced with proper alignment of the spine and pelvis. They
improve circulation, reduce fatigue, center the mind, and soothe
the nervous system. Sitting poses should be a portion of every yoga
practice. These are wonderful postures for prayer and Scripture
meditation.

Lotus Pose

1. Start in a seated position with your legs stretched out in
   front of you.
2. Place the right ankle onto the left thigh, bringing the right
   heel as close to the groin as possible. *Don't force it.* Go
   only as far as you comfortably can.
3. Soften the right kneecap toward the floor, opening the right
   hip socket.

4. LEVEL 1: Bending the left knee, rest the sole of the left foot onto the right shin. This is Half Lotus.

   LEVEL 2: Place the left ankle onto the right thigh, softening the left kneecap toward the floor, opening the left hip.

5. Hold for 4–6 breaths, then gently release. Switch your legs and repeat.

TIPS: It is crucial that you don't force this pose, since it is easy to injure yourself if you're not ready for it. Most importantly, maintain the length and integrity of the spine. Grow up and out of the hips with the crown.

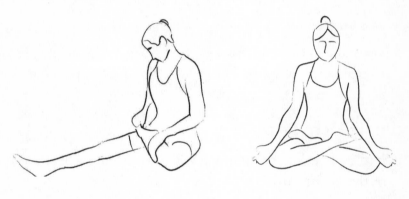

LOTUS   LOTUS 2

Hero Pose

1. Start by kneeling on your mat with the tops of the feet resting to the mat.
2. Take your hands to your calves and roll them outward, away from one another.
3. Set your tail on the floor in between your calves, using a block to sit on if it is more comfortable.
4. Relax here for 2–3 breaths, then gently release.

TIPS: You will feel this intensely in the knees, ankles, and thighs. Please be cautious.

HERO   HERO 2   HERO 3

Reclining Hero Pose

1. Start by kneeling on your mat with the tops of the feet resting on the mat.
2. Take your hands to your calves and roll them outward, away from one another.
3. Set your tail on the floor between your calves, using a block to sit on if it is more comfortable.
4. LEVEL 1: Bring your hands behind you and begin to recline the torso back toward the mat, resting on the elbows along the way.

   LEVEL 2: Rest the back flat to the mat behind you, taking your hands up overhead, lengthening the side body as much as possible.

   LEVEL 3: Take opposite hand or opposite elbow above your head and begin to really press the upper and forearms firmly into the mat, opening the chest and elevating the heart.

5. Relax here for 2–3 breaths, then gently release.

TIPS: You will feel this intensely in the knees, ankles, and thighs. Please be cautious.

RECLINING HERO

RECLINING HERO 2

RECLINING HERO 3

Seated Pigeon

1. Start in a seated position with your legs stretched out in front of you.
2. Draw the sole of the right foot toward you on the floor, placing the heel 3–5 inches from the tailbone and moving it out farther if need be.
3. Bending the left knee, place the left ankle onto the right leg, just below the knee.
4. Bring both hands behind you on to the mat and press down.
5. Hold for 4–6 breaths, then release and repeat on the other side.

TIPS: Keep your shoulders back and press your heart forward toward your right shin. You will feel this in the outer edge of your right thigh and hip. If you want more of a stretch, press your heart closer to your right shin and/or move your tail toward the left heel.

Cobbler's/Kneeling Pose

1. Kneeling on your mat, bring the inner thighs together and place the tops of your feet onto the mat.
2. Set your bottom onto your heels.
3. Keeping the spine straight, hold for 3–4 breaths and then release.

TIP: You should feel it in the tops of the feet and ankles.

COBBLER'S POSE

Cow-Face Pose

1. Start in a seated position with your legs stretched out in front of you.
2. Bend the right knee and then the left, placing the left knee on top of the right knee.

3. The right heel will be resting on the mat to the outside edge of the left hip. The left heel will be resting on the mat on the outer side of the right leg.

4. Bring the right bicep by the ear, bending at the elbow so that your fingertips rest somewhere in the middle of the upper back.

5. LEVEL 1: At the same time, bring your left arm behind your back, holding a strap between your two hands.
   LEVEL 2: Instead of using a strap, clasp your hands behind the back. Begin to move the heels away from the hips, bringing the heels in line with the knees and hinge forward.

6. Hold for 2–3 breaths and gently release. Repeat on the other side.

TIPS: The closer your heels are to your hips, the less pressure on your hip joints. Be sure that the arm that is lifted is opposite of the leg that is on top. Press the skull back into the right forearm, feeling the elbow move back and the heart and throat become more open. If you would like, hinge forward from the hips, keeping the spine straight and the chest open.

COW FACE   COW FACE 2   COW FACE 3

Simple Sitting Pose

1. Start in a sitting position with the legs outstretched in front of you.
2. Bending the right knee, bring the right sole of the foot to the inner left thigh.
3. Bend the left knee and place the left sole to the front of the right shinbone.
4. Hold for as many breaths as you like, then release and repeat other side.

TIPS: The right heel will be close to the groin, but comfortable through the ankle. Knees should be soft and the hips open. Be sure that the spine stays lengthened and the sitting bones stay rooted. This is a perfect pose for meditation.

SIMPLE SITTING

Double Pigeon Pose

1. Start in a sitting position with the legs outstretched in front of you.
2. Bend the right knee to a 90-degree angle, so that the kneecap is in line with the right hip and the right heel is in line with the kneecap.
3. Then bend the left leg as close to a 90-degree angle as is possible.
4. Place the left knee onto the right ankle and the left ankle

onto the right knee, essentially stacking opposite knee to opposite ankle.

5. LEVEL 1: Hold this position for a few breaths.
   LEVEL 2: Press a hand gently onto your left inner thigh, so that the left kneecap softens toward the mat. Hinge forward from the hips with a long, straight spine.
6. Hold for 3–5 breaths and release. Repeat on the other side.

TIPS: You will feel this immensely in your hips. Take it slow and back off a bit if needed.

DOUBLE PIGEON

Staff Pose

1. Start in a sitting position with the legs outstretched in front of you. Engage the legs by bringing the inner thighs together and flexing the toes back toward the nose.
2. You will feel your thighs press firmly into the mat as you draw your toes back. Your heels may even lift up.
3. Bring your palms alongside the body so that the heels of your hands press firmly into the mat.
4. Draw your shoulder blades back behind you, simultaneously pressing firmly into the mat with the hands.
5. You will feel your crown lift upward and your shoulders

fall away from the ears as you elevate your heart forward and upward.

6. Hold for 3–4 breaths and release. Repeat if you desire.

TIPS: Staff pose is a full body energetic pose; there's not much movement but it's very energizing. Keep your legs and core engaged, feeling every single muscle in your body working to cleanse, strengthen, and detoxify.

STAFF POSE

CHAPTER 19

Reclining and
Relaxation Postures

Let us not love with words or tongue but with actions and in truth.
This then is how we know that we belong to the truth,
and how we set our hearts at rest in his presence.
1 John 3:18—19

*R*eclining poses are generally done as a cooldown at the
end of a practice. They reduce fatigue, increase mental
clarity, and open spaces within the body that tension generally
closes. Reclining poses increase flexibility through the groin and
hips, stimulate digestion and elimination, and strengthen and
stretch the lower back and legs.

Relaxation poses soothe and balance the nervous system,
offering the body rest from physical activity. Child's Pose is used
throughout a practice whenever a rest is needed. Corpse Pose is
the quintessential restorative pose. It is typically performed at the
end of a yoga practice for deep relaxation and rejuvenation. The
Corpse Pose is often regarded the most difficult of poses because
it requires being still and receptive. It is important to take time
in both reclining and relaxation poses to breathe and completely
embrace the sensations experienced when practicing them.

Child's Pose

1. Start on all fours in Tabletop position.
2. Take your tailbone to your heels and rest the torso on the thighs.
3. Keep your arms stretched as far forward as possible, so that the body is long.
4. Tuck your tailbone toward your heels to accentuate the length in the lower back.
5. Relax for as many breaths as you like.

TIPS: You can spread the thighs wide and rest the chest toward the floor. Soften and let go of all the tension in your jaw, chest, hips, and head.

CHILD'S POSE

CHILD'S POSE-WEIGHTED

Corpse Pose

1. Lie on your back on your mat with your legs stretched out in front of you.
2. Your arms should be at your sides with palms facing upward.
3. Relax the entire body and become aware of your breath.

TIP: This is the *most important* pose in your entire practice. Take the time to be still and bask in God's presence.

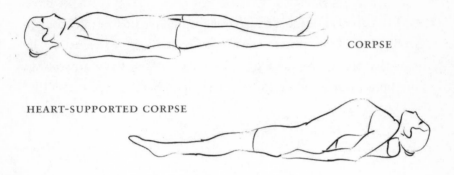

CORPSE

HEART-SUPPORTED CORPSE

Reclining Big-Toe Pose

1. Lie on your back with your legs stretched out in front of you.
2. Draw the right knee into the chest, bringing the hands just below the kneecap.
3. Keep the left leg outstretched and engaged by flexing the toes back toward the nose and the inner thigh pressing down toward the mat.
4. Begin to extend the right toes toward the ceiling, straightening the right knee.
5. Bring the hands to the back side of the right leg, either to the hamstring or the calf, and straighten the right leg as much as it allows. Flex the right foot and press the heel up toward the ceiling.
6. LEVEL 1: At the same time, drop the right hip bone back into the mat, really breathing into the back side of the knee.

   LEVEL 2: Hook the great right toe with the first two fingers and thumb of the right hand and extend the right heel high, holding onto the toe for resistance.

7. Hold for 3–5 breaths and gently release. Repeat on the other side.

TIPS: You can also drape a strap over the ball of the foot, holding on to the ends of the strap to assist in straightening the leg further. Be sure that the left hip and leg remain rooted into the mat; you can even press the left hand into the left hip to help anchor it.

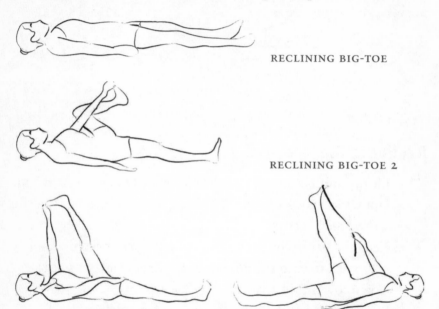

RECLINING BIG-TOE

RECLINING BIG-TOE 2

RECLINING BIG-TOE 3

RECLINING BIG-TOE WITH STRAP

Knees-to-Chest Pose

1. Lie on your back on your mat with your legs stretched out in front of you.
2. Draw the knees into the chest, bringing the hands just below the kneecaps.
3. Allow the weight of your legs to melt into the torso and chest, opening the lower back and hips.

4. Feel the weight of your arms draw your thighs closer as you drop your elbows toward the mat behind you.

5. Hold for 3–4 breaths and release. Repeat as often as you like.

TIPS: You can rock back and forth lightly and/or take small circles left and right to massage the lower back. This is a great pose to use in between back bends to reset the spine.

KNEES-TO-CHEST

Bound-Angle Pose

1. Lie on your back with your legs stretched out in front of you.

2. Bending the knees, bring the soles of your feet together so that the heels are somewhat close to the groin. Soften your knees outward and downward toward the mat, opening the hips, lower back, and belly.

3. LEVEL 1: Relax in this position.
   LEVEL 2: Press the great toes firmly into one another and then toward the mat, lifting the heels slightly to get a little deeper into your hips.

4. Breathe and repeat as often as you like.

TIPS: Allow the entire soles of the feet to touch one another. This is a great pose to use in between back bends to reset the spine.

BOUND-ANGLE POSE

Lying Spinal Twist (with Variation)

1. Start lying flat on your mat with your legs outstretched. Draw both knees into your chest, draping the hands just below your knees so that the tops of the thighs soften into the belly and chest.

2. Open your arms out like wings, pressing the palms into the mat.

3. Bring your knees to a 90-degree angle, so that the knees stack over the hips and the heels are in line with the knees.

4. Draw the inner thighs tightly toward one another and then drop both knees to the right. Hold for 1–2 breaths.

5. LEVEL 1: Bring knees back to center, using your core strength, then drop them to the left and hold for 1–2 breaths.

   LEVEL 2: When dropping the knees to the right and left, keep the knees and thighs elevated off of the mat an inch or two on each side, using your core strength to keep the legs lifted.

6. Draw the knees back into the chest when finished, rocking back and forth on the mat to massage the lower back.

LYING SPINAL TWIST

LYING SPINAL TWIST 2

One-Leg Variation

1. While lying flat on the mat, bring just the right knee in to the chest, keeping the left leg outstretched.
2. Engage the left leg by flexing the toes back toward the nose and anchoring the left inner thigh down toward the mat.
3. Open the arms out like wings and drop the right knee over to the left side of the body.
4. You can rest the left hand on the right knee if you would like, keeping the left lung lifting upward.
5. Hold for 3–5 breaths, then repeat on the other side.

LYING SPINAL
TWIST VARIATION

CHAPTER 20

Routines

Morning

This routine is a nice way to warm up your body after a good night's rest. Take your time during this series. It is a strengthening series that requires a good amount of focus to complete initially. Be sure to breathe for at least 2–3 breaths in each pose. Once you have practiced it awhile and feel comfortable, you can add additional poses from the posture chapters to give your body some variety.

- Mountain

- Arms up—hinge to right and left

- Forward Fold

- Halfway Lift

- Forward Fold

- Halfway Lift

- Forward Fold

- Sweep up to standing with arms up—
  hinge to right and left

- Right Leg—Warrior 1

- Right Leg—Warrior 2

- Top of a Push-Up

- Downward Facing Dog

- Step forward to Forward Fold

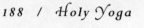

- Sweep up to standing with arms up— hinge to right and left

- Left Leg—Warrior 1

- Left Leg—Warrior 2

- Top of a Push-Up

- Downward Facing Dog

- Step forward to a Forward Fold

- Camel Pose

- Cat/Cow Pose

- Camel Pose

- Cat/Cow Pose

- Headstand—Please skip if you are not ready for one

- Pigeon Pose on the right

- Pigeon Pose on the left

- High Push-Up

- Downward Facing Dog

- Step the feet forward to a Forward Fold

- Sweep up to standing

- Close in Mountain with your hands in prayer at your heart center

- Either lie or sit comfortably on your mat for 5–10 minutes of meditation.

Gentle

This is a great series to practice if you are new to yoga, or if you simply want a gentler experience. Gentle classes are the best time to sit with God and experience Him through your very deliberate intention of doing so. Poses in this series are strung together to softly address all parts of the physical form. Take 3–5 breaths in each pose, making sure that you take the time to feel the pose. You need to feel in order to heal, physically, emotionally, or spiritually. This series can be done anytime, day or night. Once you feel comfortable, please refer back to the posture chapters to add and remove poses that challenge you in growth.

- Start seated

- Neck rolls

- Cow-Face Pose—both sides

- Seated Pigeon

- Knees to Chest

- Reclining Big Toe—both sides

- Bridge Pose

- Reclining Bound Angle—no props

- Fish Pose

- Cat/Cow Pose

- Child's Pose

- Downward Facing Dog

- Plank Pose with knees dropped

- Lie on belly

- Sphinx

- Lie on Belly

- Cobra

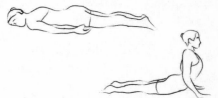

- Child's Pose

- Corpse Pose for 5–10 minute
  meditation

Flow Sequences

The following flows are the standard series that you would find in any flow (or "vinyasa") class anywhere, so I thought them important to give you. They are traditionally called Sun Series A and Sun Series B. In Holy Yoga we refer to them appropriately as *Son* Series A and B. These are much quicker routines to follow and are designed to energize the body. Each movement is given one part of the breath, as you will see noted alongside the name of the pose. Son Series can be your entire practice, or it can be woven into a class, as you will see outlined in the Level 2 routine here. These are not to be done when first beginning your Holy Yoga practice. Give yourself time to learn the basics, establishing good alignment and breath control, and then move on to using these.

Son Series A

- Mountain Pose—Inhale

- Standing Forward Fold—Exhale

- Lift halfway up—Inhale

- Plank Pose—exhale and inhale

- Yoga Push-Up—exhale

- Cobra/Upward Facing Dog—inhale

- Downward Facing Dog—exhale and breathe 3–5 breaths

- Step both feet forward to Standing Forward Fold—exhale

- Sweep arms up to Mountain—inhale

- Repeat if you desire

Son Series B

- Mountain Pose—inhale

- Chair Pose—exhale/inhale

- Standing Forward Fold—exhale

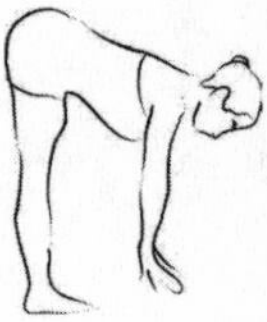

- Lift halfway up—inhale

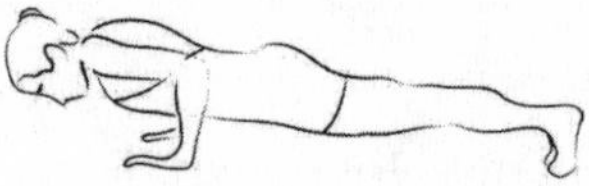

- Yoga Push-Up—exhale

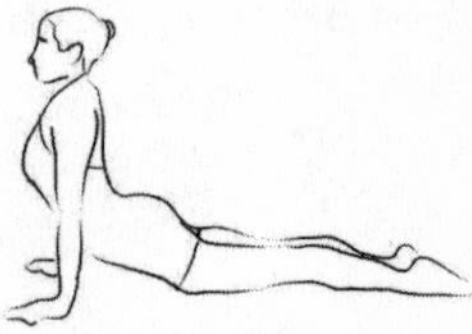

- Cobra/Upward Facing Dog—inhale

- Downward Facing Dog—exhale

- Right Foot Warrior 1—inhale

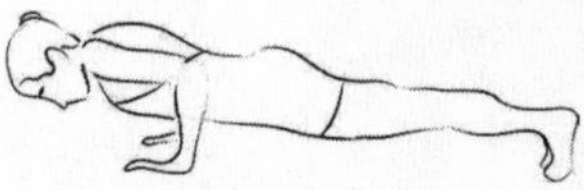

- Yoga Push-Up—exhale

- Cobra/Upward Facing Dog— inhale

- Downward Facing Dog— exhale

- Left Foot Warrior 1—inhale

- Yoga Push-Up—exhale

- Cobra/Upward Facing Dog— inhale

- Downward Facing Dog

- Step both feet forward to Standing Forward Fold—exhale

- Chair Pose—inhale/exhale

- Mountain Pose—inhale/exhale

- Repeat if you desire

Level 2

This is a more advanced series you should use if you are somewhat experienced with yoga. It is challenging and active—get ready to sweat! You will practice the Son Series with quicker breath flow, but the other poses will be a three-breath hold. Do not do the entire routine if you feel unable. Break it into sections and work up to a full Level 2 routine. As with the rest of the routines, you can refer back to the posture chapters to add variations at any time. Be sure that you vary a standing pose with another standing pose, a forward bend with another forward bend, and so on.

- Son Series A or B, 2–3 times

- Downward Facing Dog

- Right Foot Lunge

- Right Side Crescent Pose

- Right Side Crescent Twist

- Plank Pose

- Upward Facing Dog

- Downward Facing Dog

- Left Foot Lunge

- Left Side Crescent Pose

- Left Side Crescent Twist

- Plank Pose

- Upward Facing Dog

- Downward Facing Dog

- Right Foot Warrior 1

- Right Foot Warrior 2

- Right Side Extended Angle

- Right Side Triangle

- Right Side Pyramid

- Standing Forward Fold

- Son Series A

- Downward Facing Dog

- Left Side Warrior 1

- Left Side Warrior 2

- Left Side Extended Angle

- Left Side Triangle

- Left Side Pyramid

- Standing Forward Fold

- Sweep up to Mountain

- Tree Pose right then left

- Seated Pigeon right then left

- Lying Spinal Twist right then left

- Knees to Chest

- Shoulder Stand or Legs-Up-the-Wall

- Plow

- Fish Pose

- Corpse Pose for a 5–10 minute meditation

Evening

There is nothing better than a calming practice in the evening. It relaxes the body and helps you process the day's events. It will help you get a good night's sleep by preparing your mind for rest. This is a shorter routine. Please allow time for about five breaths per pose. As with other routines, please feel free to refer back to the posture chapters to add variations. Be sure to keep your substitutions at the same length and exertion level. This is a routine meant to calm and soothe the body. Avoid practicing inversions and backward bending postures in the evening, as they tend to excite the nervous system and awaken the body.

- Start lying in Corpse Pose

- Knees to Chest

- Reclining Big Toe Pose, right then left

- Bridge Pose (just to work out the kinks in the lower back)

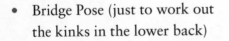

- Lying Twist to right and left

- Cat/Cow Pose

- Downward Facing Dog

- Child's Pose

- Downward Facing Dog

- Warrior 1 Right Side

- Lunge Right Side

- Plank Pose

- Downward Facing Dog

- Warrior 1 Left Side

- Lunge Left Side

- Plank Pose

- Downward Facing Dog

- Child's Pose

- Reclining Hero Pose

- Seated Pigeon—right side then left

- Gentle Spinal Twist 1—
  right side then left

- Seated Forward Fold

- Knees to Chest

- Corpse Pose for a 5–10 minute
  meditation

Restorative

This routine may seem easy, but it may prove to be the most challenging of the lot. These poses require patience and proper preparation. They are designed to nourish and rest the body on a very deep level. The poses are usually held for several minutes at a time, five to ten minutes per pose in general, and never more than fifteen minutes. It is important to start off with a few light stretches, like Cat/Cow or Downward Facing Dog, just to shed the restlessness in the physical body in preparation for these very deep and prayerful poses.

Take the time to support the body in appropriate ways in order to really release the underlying tension deep in joints and muscles. While there may only be four or five poses, a restorative routine should take you about thirty to forty minutes to complete.

Remember your breath and have your Scripture passages ready if you would like to meditate on them. (If you feel led to restorative yoga, a great book is *Relax and Renew* by Judith Lasater. As with all traditional yoga books, apply the Holy Yoga philosophy to the poses.)

Legs-Up-the-Wall Pose

Roll a small towel and place under your neck to ensure that the natural curve in your neck is supported. Using a folded blanket or a bolster, elevate your hips slightly as you walk your feet up the wall. Leave your hips elevated for the duration of the pose. You can bolster your heart as in Supported Corpse if desired. Use an eye pillow or small towel over your eyes if you like, to enhance relaxation. You can place a small weight [sand, sugar, or flour bag] on the soles of the feet if you choose, helping to open the soles of the feet and calves.

Reclining Bound Angle

Roll a small towel and place under your neck to ensure that the natural curve in your neck is supported. Use a blanket folded lengthwise or a bolster between the shoulder blades to elevate the heart as in Supported Corpse. You can use an eye pillow or small towel over your eyes if you like, to help enhance relaxation. Some restorative teachers say that a strap wrapped around the feet and lower back is a necessary component to the pose. See how it feels for you.

Child's Pose—Weighted

Have the thighs spread wide so that the heart can soften. You can place a bolster between the legs, resting the chest on it if you like. You can also place some sort of light weight on the lower back to keep the tail moving toward the floor. You can use a yoga sandbag, or a small bag of flour or sugar from your baking cupboard.

Heart-Supported Corpse Pose

Place a bolster lengthwise between the shoulder blades, elevating the heart. You can use an eye pillow or small towel over your eyes if you like, to help enhance relaxation.

Supported Bridge Pose

Roll a small towel and place under your neck to ensure that the natural curve in your neck is supported. Place a block under your sacrum so that the sacrum is resting on the block. You can use the block at whatever height feels most comfortable to you.

You can use an eye pillow or small towel over your eyes if you like, to help enhance relaxation.

Pregnancy

While there are specific classes designed for pre- and postnatal participation, the key to any pregnancy-related class is to understand the precautions and modifications associated with them. You can do any series of poses with modifications just as long as you keep the following blanket rules in mind. If you have previous experience with yoga and become pregnant, please modify your practice according to the way that you feel. If you are wanting to learn yoga for the first time because you are pregnant, pay very close attention to the following precautions. Once you understand the precautions, you can use poses from the posture chapters to guide you through a personalized practice.

- Preparing your body for labor and motherhood is the goal of establishing a yoga practice. Using the breathing techniques associated with yoga can help you in the labor and delivery process.
- If you are brand-new to yoga, I strongly recommend finding a prenatal class near you to learn the poses and modifications associated with a safe pre- and postnatal practice. I stress learning the poses only. Be sure to communicate to your instructor how you feel about traditional yoga philosophy and express that your interest is strictly in safety. Once you learn, you can make your practice Holy Yoga using the principles outlined in this book.
- If you are a yoga practitioner, you can continue to practice only with modifications during the first trimester. If you are new to the practice, avoid starting until you are in your

second trimester. It is important to be very gentle with yourself during that critical first twelve weeks while your baby is setting roots for healthy gestation in the womb.

- During pregnancy the body produces the hormone relaxin, which softens the connective tissue. The good news is that this allows the pelvic joints to become more flexible while the uterus expands, making space for the baby. The bad news is that it can lead to instability in the sacroiliac joints and can cause lower back pain, so pregnant women need to be careful not to overstretch in their poses. While you're pregnant, it is important not to strive for flexibility, although it may happen as a result of hormonal surges and swings.

- Breathing is the most essential part of a pregnancy-related practice. Use the Focused Breath—a long, strong, deep breath that helps you to focus on the present moment and maintain calm, and Alternate Nostril Breathing (ANB), which helps to balance the body's energy flows. Avoid any kind of breath retention or hyperventilation that could limit the baby's oxygen supply. As correct deep breathing nurtures the circulatory, cardiovascular, endocrine, digestive, and nervous systems, sleep comes more easily and moodiness can be less problematic.

- During pregnancy, the volume of blood in the body expands 40 to 60 percent to support the fetus and placenta. The blood circulates faster, the rate of metabolism increases, and the resting heart rate rises. You're using up your body's sugar faster, as important reserves are being used to support the placenta and fetus. To meet the needs of your changing metabolism, eat a light meal or snack about an hour before class, drink plenty of liquids, and don't push yourself too much.

- *Do not* practice any inversions or full back bends. Avoid lying on your back after the first trimester as the weight of the baby can restrict blood flow to the fetus and leave you and your baby feeling dizzy and nauseous. Lie on your left side for Corpse Pose.

- Support your lower back and pelvis with blocks, blankets, and bolsters to ensure proper alignment and avoid too much pressure on the joints.

- In Child's Pose, be sure to spread the thighs wide, allowing for your belly to rest on the floor while supported by the thighs alongside the side body. This will be great for releasing tension in your lower back and knees.

For Further Reference

Here are a few books I recommend if you'd like to discover more about yoga, the mind/body connection, or about Christian meditation.

An Invitation to Christian Yoga
Nancy Roth

Celebration of Discipline
Richard Foster

Hatha Yoga Illustrated
Brooke Boon and Martin Kirk

Prayer of Heart and Mind
Thomas Ryan

Reclaiming the Body in Christian Spirituality
Thomas Ryan

Relax and Renew: Restful Yoga for Stressful Times
Judith Lasater, PhD

Savoring God's Word: Cultivating the Soul-Transforming Practice of Scripture Meditation
Jan Johnson

Yoga for Christians
Susan Bordenkircher

Yoga Rx
Larry Payne, PhD and Richard Usatine, MD

Notes

INTRODUCTION

1. *Random House Webster's Unabridged Dictionary,* 2nd ed. (New York: Random House, 2001), 912.

CHAPTER 1

1. "General Yoga Information/History of Yoga," American Yoga Association Web site: http://www.americanyogaassociation.org/general.html.
2. Larry Payne, PhD, and Richard Usatine, MD, *Yoga Rx* (New York: Broadway Books, 2002), 5.
3. Payne and Usatine, *Yoga Rx,* 4.
4. Georg Feuerstein, PhD, and Larry Payne, PhD, *Yoga for Dummies* (Foster City, CA: IDG Books Worldwide, Inc., 1999), 21.

CHAPTER 2

1. Thomas Ryan, *Prayer of Heart and Body* (New York: Paulist Press, 1995), 149.
2. Richard J. Foster, *Celebration of Discipline* (San Francisco: Harper & Row, 1978), 1.
3. Ibid., 6.
4. Jerry Bridges, *The Pursuit of Holiness* (Colorado Springs: NavPress, 1978), 96.
5. Frederica Mathewes-Green, *The Open Door* (Brewster, MA: Paraclete Press, 2003), 102.

6. Hank Hanegraaff, *The Prayer of Jesus* (Nashville: Word Publishing, 2001), 9.

7. Ryan, *Prayer of Heart*, 127.

8. Doug Pagitt and Kathryn Prill, *Body Prayer* (Colorado Springs: Waterbrook Press, 2005), 6.

CHAPTER 3

1. Bob Rognlien, *Experiential Worship* (Colorado Springs: NavPress, 2005), 35–41.

2. Ibid.

3. Chris Armstrong, "Embrace Your Inner Pentecostal," *Christianity Today,* September 2006, 86.

4. Nancy Roth, *An Invitation to Christian Yoga* (New York: Seabury Books, 2005), 2.

5. Rognlien, *Experiential*, 40.

6. Lauren Winner, *Mudhouse Sabbath* (Brewster, MA: Paraclete Press, 2003), 67.

7. Pagitt and Prill, *Body Prayer*, 3.

8. Rognlien, *Experiential*, 63.

9. Roth, *Invitation*, 2.

CHAPTER 4

1. Roth, *Invitation*, 7.

CHAPTER 5

1. Payne and Usatine, *Yoga Rx*, 7.

2. Robert Elmer, *Practicing God's Presence* (Colorado Springs: NavPress, 2005), 46.

3. Ibid., 72.

4. Charles Ringma, *Mother Teresa* (Colorado Springs: NavPress, 2004), Reflection 35.

5. Mark Buchanan, *The Rest of God* (Nashville: W Publishing Group, 2006), 5.

6. Elmer, *Practicing*, 53.

7. Kathleen Norris, *Amazing Grace* (New York: Riverhead Books, 1998), 61.

8. Bridges, *Pursuit,* 81.

9. The Quotable Christian, http://www.pietyhilldesign.com/gcq/ quotepages/obedience.html

CHAPTER 6

1. Carol Sorgen, "Yoga for Men," Web MD, http://www.webmd.com/ content/Article/58/66562.htm?pagenumber=2

2. Frederic Luskin, "Just Relax!" *Parade,* September 24, 2006, 16.

3. Rich Weil, "Strike a Pose," Web MD, http://www.webmd.com/ content/article/111/109846.htm

4. Brenton Diaz, "Christianity and Stress," *Relevant Magazine,* September 2005, http://www.relevantmagazine.com/beta/life_ article.php?id=7019

5. Sorgen, "Yoga for Men," http://www.webmd.com/content/ Article/58/66562.htm?pagenumber=3

6. Payne and Usatine, *Yoga Rx,* 100–104.

7. Ibid., 157–158.

8. Louise Rafkin, "Stay Young with Yoga," WebMD, http://www .webmd.com/content/article/12/1738_50707.htm

9. Ibid.

CHAPTER 9

1. Hanegraaff, *Prayer,* 85.

2. Ryan, *Prayer,* 28.

3. Thomas à Kempis, *Of the Imitation of Christ* (New Canaan, CT: Keats Publishing, 1973), 79.

4. Foster, *Celebration,* 23.

5. Ryan, *Prayer,* 15.

6. Foster, *Celebration,* 22.

7. Ibid., 13.

Posture Index

About the Author

BROOKE BOON (E-RYT, CYT) is the founder of Holy Yoga. She is an energetic and dedicated lover of the Lord, the Word, and yoga. She creatively weaves spirituality, physical alignment, practical wisdom, and the Word into the fabric of her teaching. She has been blessed with the opportunity to be a leader in the Christian yoga movement while developing and implementing Holy Yoga practices around the globe.

Brooke created and facilitates the Holy Yoga Teacher Training Program, which trains devoted believers to inspire students to connect individually to Christ through the worship of Holy Yoga.

Brooke has a deep appreciation for the practice of yoga and connection to Christ as a collective and authentic path to wellness. "The love of the Lord and His Word has given this practice its power, flow, and grace. It is like nothing I have ever taught or been taught. It is a true form of worship."

Brooke coauthored *Hatha Yoga Illustrated,* which was published and internationally released in January 2004. Brooke lives in Phoenix, Arizona, with her husband, Jarrett, and three children: Jory, Jace, and Brynn. You can visit her Web site at www.holyyoga.net.

Interested in Becoming a
Holy Yoga Instructor?

❧

Holy Yoga was created to introduce physical worship of the Lord through prayer, breath, and movement to all seekers of and believers in Jesus Christ, regardless of denomination. The purpose of the ministry is to introduce people to yoga as a form of collective (mind, body, and spirit) worship. Holy Yoga is dedicated to educating students and certifying teachers through the school of Holy Yoga to facilitate Christ-centered classes in their individual churches, studios, and spaces worldwide.

The Holy Yoga Teacher Training Program is a two-hundred-hour certification that will be submitted upon completion to the Yoga Alliance for registration as an RYT (registered yoga teacher). Upon completion, you will be a Holy Yoga CYT (Certified Yoga Teacher) and eligible to register as an RYT (Registered Yoga Teacher) through the Yoga Alliance. Having an RYT affiliation deems the certification safe and insurable. Holy Yoga is an internationally recognized RYS (Registered Yoga School) through the Yoga Alliance. The minimum teaching requirement is two hundred hours. This program's entire hours will generate credit toward a five-hundred-hour certification if the student desires to attain one.

This program is a commitment to glorifying God through yoga. We have a passion for serving Him by teaching how to authentically connect to Christ in worship and praise using all our heart, souls, minds, and strength.

Holy Yoga offers two-hundred-hour accreditation trainings two to three times annually online and in retreat locales in the U.S. and Mexico. If you are interested in bringing this ministry to your area, please contact 866-737-HOLY or visit us on the Web at www.holyyoga.net.